The Soul
Renew Your Mind to Save Your Soul

By:

Rev. Ricky Edwards

"The Word is Eternal" Isaiah 40:8

Printed in the United States of America

Published by Aion Multimedia
20118 N 67th Ave
Suite 300-446
Glendale AZ 85308
www.aionmultimedia.com

ISBN: 978-0-9976046-4-1

Table of Contents

James 1:21 (KJV)

21 Wherefore lay apart all filthiness and superfluity of naughtiness, and receive with meekness the engrafted word, which is able to save your souls.

Acknowledgements

I would like to thank my wife, Sally, for standing at my side these past 36 years. You have always been willing to go and do whatever God led us into.

Also, thank you to Pastor Mark and Brenda Thomas, who supported us from the very beginning of our walk with God since 1984.

Preface

On the day of salvation, when our spirit is saved, our name is written in the *Lamb's Book of Life*. We call this being born again spiritually. At that time, we receive a whole new glory land that outshines the sun. We're looking forward to going to Heaven, but we've still got a lot of work to do here on Earth. So, we cannot just live life any old way we want until we get to Heaven. We need to glean enough information from the WORD of God so we can live victoriously here in this life before we ever go to Heaven. You see, we don't just look to Heaven as a future place of victory. Heaven is also receiving Jesus and living victoriously on Earth here *in this life now*. Understanding the difference between saving the spirit and saving the soul is a key to living victoriously now.

As I was meditating on this truth, I came to realize that there are two areas in which Christians tend to struggle consistently. Most everyone agrees, all Christians have to deal with the devil. But, would we also agree, all Christians have to deal with themselves? By that, I mean their soul and their body. Some time ago, my wife, Pastor Sally, and I were on the road ministering for quite a while. During these trips, I was listening to some messages on this topic by Brother Kenneth E. Hagin, the founder of Rhema Bible Training Center in Broken Arrow, Oklahoma (now called Rhema Bible Training College or "Rhema" for short). As I mediated on, and prayed about, what I was hearing, the LORD began teaching me more about ministering to Christians who have difficulty with these areas of their lives – areas of the flesh and soulish realm. He said, "When you get home, teach this." I've been teaching it ever since and this book is a product of that teaching.

Helpful Formatting Notes

It is often helpful to understand the thought processes behind the layout of a book of this nature. We have broken each chapter up into smaller more manageable sections. Don't worry about reading a whole chapter in one sitting. Allow yourself to feed on one section at a time and truly digest this material.

Because we believe all Scripture is the inerrant WORD of God and Jesus is the very LOGOS (3056.Logos) or divine utterance of God[1], you will see that we capitalize the entire word "WORD" when referring to the WORD of God. Along the same lines, the word "LORD" is also completely capitalized to honor Jesus as the one who paid the ransom for our spirits with His very blood (2962.Kurios). Additionally, all pronouns referring to God, Holy Spirit, and Jesus are capitalized as well.

Scriptures are handled four ways in this book:

1. The main Scripture references discussed are inset from both margins and displayed in *italics* with important phrases ***bolded***.

2. Other Scriptures, if quoted exactly are shown in quotations and italics, and are usually found within the paragraph itself.

3. If Scriptures are paraphrased they are given in quotations, but not shown in italics. The reference will be given in the footnotes.

4. When Scriptural proof is presented for a doctrinal statement, the appropriate Scripture references are usually listed in a footnote on the same page.

---

[1] John 1:1-16

It is important to note, we have endeavored to list a reference for every Scripture whether directly quoted or paraphrased because our goal is to be as scripturally accurate as possible. We have also endeavored to provide a complete bibliography should you wish to dig deeper into any of these subjects.

Introduction

Jesus did a lot of teaching because it is such an important part of ministry. Teaching is expounding upon the WORD line upon line and precept upon precept – it's like building a house one brick at a time. You see it is often in the teaching when light, revelation, and illumination come to increase knowledge and faith. When knowledge and faith are increased, the potential to walk in victory is also increased.

The Importance of Teaching

In John 14:12, Jesus said there are greater works that you and I, as believers, would do because He was leaving; and, of course, we know He did leave. So what exactly does this mean that believers can do greater works than Jesus did? Well, I don't believe we can do better, in terms of quality, than the works Jesus did. But, because there are so many more of us now, I believe we can do greater works in terms of quantity. Let me show you what I mean.

> *12 Verily, verily, I say unto you, He that believeth on me, the works that I do shall he do also; and **greater works than these shall he do**; because I go unto my Father. (John 14:12, KJV, emphasis added)*

> *7 Nevertheless I tell you the truth; It is **expedient for you that I go away**: for if I go not away, the Comforter will not come unto you; but if I depart, I will*

send him unto you. (John 16:7, KJV,
emphasis added)

First, we must establish who Jesus is speaking to in John chapters 14 and 16. In this case, He is speaking to the disciples who represent the church. Second, we know that when Jesus left, He became the first begotten from the dead[2]. Third, Paul received the revelation that once Jesus died and rose again, He was no longer *the Body of Christ*, but instead became the *Head of the Body of Christ*[3]. Finally, from I Cor 12:12, we know there's only one *Body*, but it has many *members*. Putting all of this together, we now understand that when Jesus became the *Head*, all of the believers became the *Body*. In other words, we can understand John 14:12 as saying, "...the works that I do shall *you (e.g., Ricky, and Julie, and Tom, and all the members of the Church universal)* do also; and greater works than these shall *you* do; because I go unto my Father." Therefore, we can do more in terms of *quantity* than Jesus did because there are so many more of us to do the works of Jesus now. However, I don't believe anyone can do anything better than He did in terms of *quality*.

But there is a little more to this. We have to understand why we are able to do these things as the Body of Christ. When Jesus was here on Earth, He was the Body of Christ. But, as He was preparing to leave this Earth, He understood He was going to die a sinner's death. Yet He had never sinned. He wasn't dying because of His own sin. He was going to die a sinner's death because He was taking our sin. He did this so we could be saved. So, when He said we would do greater works than He, because He was going to His Father, He was also explaining that we would then have the

---

2 Revelation 1:5

3 Colossians 1:18

2

ability to be spiritually saved. In other words, the opportunity for greater works comes as a result of spiritual salvation.

Therefore, if we are going to do what Jesus did and more, we need to understand exactly how He conducted His ministry here on Earth so we can pattern our ministry after His. From reading about Jesus in the Gospels, we see most of the time He used the same pattern before He ever ministered healing to anyone. Let's look at Luke 6:18 in the New Living Translation ("NLT") as an example:

> [18] *They had come **to hear** him and **to be healed** of their diseases; and those troubled by evil spirits **were healed**. (Luke 6:18, NLT, emphasis added)*

From this verse can you tell His pattern? Remember, nothing in the Bible is random. This verse is written in a specific order because it happened in that order and the order is important. First it says, "…*they came to hear Him*," and then it says, "…*to be healed*." If they came to hear Him first then He must have been teaching first. Why would He do that? So faith would come. If people don't know what belongs to them, then they won't have faith to go after it. Let's look at a few more Scriptural witnesses:

> [2] *And when the Sabbath day was come, he began to **teach** in the synagogue: and many hearing him were astonished, saying, "From whence hath this man these things and what wisdom is this which is given unto him, that even such mighty works are wrought by his hands?"*
>
> [6] *And he marveled because of their **unbelief**. And he went round about the villages, **teaching**. (Mark 6:2 &6, KJV, emphasis added)*

It is important to notice when Jesus encountered unbelief He would begin teaching. Remember, the Law of Faith says that believing comes by hearing and hearing by the WORD of God[4]. He overcame their unbelief by teaching them the WORD. Jesus was always consistent. There are about 15 places in the Gospels that show us where Jesus taught, or preached, or both first, and then He healed. Let's look at a couple more:

> [23] *And Jesus went about all Galilee, **teaching** in their synagogues, and **preaching** the gospel of the kingdom, and **healing** all manner of sickness and all manner of disease among the people. (Matthew 4:23, KJV, emphasis added)*

> [35] *And Jesus went about all the cities and villages, **teaching** in their synagogues, and **preaching** the gospel of the kingdom, and **healing** every sickness and every disease among the people. (Matthew 9:35, KJV, emphasis added)*

Normally, when people think of healing, they think of someone coming up out of a wheelchair, or blind eyes opening. But there's more to it. Sometimes healing is a process during which someone has to use their faith over a period of time. That's why the teaching is so important. If they aren't taught, they won't know how to walk it out.

Many times when we travel, the LORD will tell us before we get to a place, "I want you to teach for several days before you minister to the people." When we are obedient to follow the Holy Ghost, we always see Him working. Sometimes people are healed instantly and sometimes slowly. We rejoice the same either way, because the healing always comes. Praise God!

---

4 Romans 10:17

I remember there was a deaf boy one time, I don't remember how old he was – maybe 10 or so. His mom brought him up for prayer. We were there at the church and the power of God came. The boy was completely healed and his mom got so excited, she grabbed his face, "Can you hear me?"

"Yeah," the boy replied. His mom got all excited and stirred up. That's wonderful, but the big deal of it is not just *getting* somebody healed or delivered, its *keeping* them healed and delivered.

You never want somebody to get healed, and then allow the devil to come along with thoughts and talk them out of their healing. If that happens, it's harder to get them back to a place of victory. That's why I continually teach people who they are in Christ, and what belongs to them as children of God. I want to make sure that once they're healed, they'll know how to stay healed – because *staying healed* is walking in victory!

The Devil Moves in Ignorance

So what are the three things that Jesus did? Teach, preach, and heal. Therefore, in doing the works of Jesus, we'll be safe if we pattern our lives that way – teaching, preaching, and healing. The problem is people don't always see the teaching part of ministry as the works of Jesus. Sometimes they only consider the manifestation of the miraculous as the works of Jesus – even though Jesus did quite a lot of teaching.

In Romans 10:14, Paul wrote, "How can they believe in whom they've not heard?" And then in verse 17 it says, *"Faith comes by hearing and hearing by the WORD of God" (New King James Version "NKJV")* so what we believe now is always based upon what we have once heard. In addition, whatever part of the WORD I believe will have a corresponding action to go with it, because faith without works is dead[5].

Another reason we teach, as I mentioned before, is because the devil moves in ignorance. The revelation and knowledge that teaching brings shuts the devil down. He cannot move where knowledge has brought light and understanding.

When I was a kid growing up, I remember people used to quote some of the Old Covenant language such as, *"Though The LORD slay me, yet will I serve Him" (Job 13:15, KJV).* You know, it is commendable to love God in such a way that you will serve Him even if you believe He is making you sick or trying to kill you. But according to the New Testament, it shows a lack of knowledge and that's exactly the place where the devil wants to keep as many people as possible[6]. However, with the New Testament and many great teachers and preachers along the way, we now understand that God isn't mad at folk, He doesn't put sickness on people, and He certainly doesn't want to kill anyone. God loves humanity. That is the kind of knowledge that shuts the devil down.

The Role of Honor

When teaching about doing the works of Jesus, sometimes I get tickled. People will make statements along the lines of, "Well, if you worked like Jesus, then you'd just heal everybody." Really? Well, you must not have read the four gospels if you believe that. Because there are several cases where Jesus didn't get everyone

---

[5] James 2:17

[6] Hosea 4:6

healed, and it wasn't due to a lack of anointing, since the Bible records that He had the Holy Spirit without measure[7]. For example, in Luke 8, the woman with the issue of blood wasn't the only one who touched Jesus that day, yet the Bible clearly records that she was the only one who received healing virtue from Him in the press[8].

Jesus' own hometown of Nazareth is another example.

>*[1]And he went out from thence, and came into his own country; and his disciples followed him.*

>*[2] And when the Sabbath day was come, he began to teach in the synagogue: and many hearing him were astonished, saying, From whence hath this man these things? and what wisdom is this which is given unto him, that even such mighty works are wrought by his hands?*

>*[3] Is not this the carpenter, the son of Mary, the brother of James, and Joses, and of Juda, and Simon? and are not his sisters here with us? And they were offended at him.*

>*[4] But Jesus, said unto them, **A prophet is not without honour, but in his own country, and among his own kin, and in his own house.***

>*[5] **And he could there do no mighty work, save that he laid his hands upon a few sick folk, and healed them.***

>*[6] And he marveled because of their unbelief. And he went round about the*

---

villages, teaching. (Mark 6:1-6, KJV, emphasis added)

Listen carefully here, in order to receive from someone or, more specifically to receive from God, there must be faith and also an understanding of honor. Jesus is showing us in Mark 6 how the degree of honor we give the WORD of God **and** the *man or woman of God* affects our ability to receive from God.

In verse four Jesus said, *"...A prophet is not without honor but in his own country...And he could do no mighty work save that he laid his hand upon a few sick folk and he healed them..."* Jesus didn't get as far with the manifestations of people being healed and delivered as he wanted in Nazareth. They just wouldn't receive it because the people didn't understand some things about honor. So, He would teach, preach, and heal. We see it in verse six, *"And he marveled because of their unbelief. And he went round about the villages, teaching."*

Most men in the generation before me, those who grew up during the great wars, had a keen understanding of the importance of honor from a natural perspective. Brother Kenneth E. Hagin was one of those who also understood the importance of honor from the spiritual perspective. In 1950, God mandated him to teach faith. Many years later, as part of that mandate, he founded Rhema Bible Training College ("Rhema") in Broken Arrow, Oklahoma. My wife, Sally, and I had the honor of attending Rhema in the late 80s. Most of the stories I share about Brother Hagin, I share from firsthand knowledge because I sat under him as a student for so long.

Jesus visited Brother Hagin several times over the course of his lifetime. One time, when Jesus appeared to him, He told Brother Hagin, "Doubt is not necessarily because you don't believe. It is mistrust because there's not confidence in something different." To replace something that supports what you and I think, we must be taught something else that replaces what we currently believe and how we currently look at things. We want to replace our old thinking with the WORD of God so that we learn new things and keep moving forward from glory to glory.

When Jesus appeared to Brother Hagin, He also said the number one way to cure unbelief and doubt is always teaching. In Mark 6, Jesus was doing healings and didn't get the results he wanted so he stopped doing that and started teaching the WORD.

Let's look at Matthew 4:23 and 9:35 again.

> 23 And Jesus went about all Galilee, teaching in their synagogues, and preaching the gospel of the kingdom, and healing **all manner of sickness and all manner of disease among the people**. *(Matthew 4:23, KJV, emphasis added)*
>
> 35 And Jesus went about all the cities and villages, teaching in their synagogues, and preaching the gospel of the kingdom, and **healing every sickness and every disease among the people**. *(Matthew 9:35, KJV, emphasis added)*

Jesus went about teaching and preaching the gospel of the kingdom, healing every sickness and disease among the people. Those verses do not say that He healed *every individual person*; rather, *each disease that was present among the people was taken care of.* It was up to the people to believe healing power was present to heal them, and to either receive it by faith, or to reject it in unbelief. The honor they gave to Jesus as a man of God had a direct bearing on their faith – whether they would believe that He had indeed taken care of that disease or not.

Teaching Helps People Keep Their Healing

The woman with the issue of blood, and a few others in the Bible, are exceptions where Jesus did not have to teach first. She came with her faith gun loaded. She already honored Him as the Healer and she pulled the trigger on her faith the minute she touched Him. But on the whole, everywhere else in the Bible, before Jesus did much healing, He would always teach a Bible lesson. He would either teach or preach and then a demonstration would follow – sometimes with laying on of hands and sometimes not – but the power of God was always there to transform lives.

It's the same today, when you go to church and your pastor is teaching a good solid Bible lesson, he is doing the works of Jesus. Whether anyone lays hands on you in a service or not, the power of God is still there to transform your life if you will believe it and receive it. Even while you are reading this book, the power of God is available to transform you.

Sometimes I remember back to when we first moved to Southeast Texas in the summer of 1988. Our church was a little 20'x20' portable building. The people would come and they would say the anointing wasn't as strong when I started teaching as it was when I was preaching. All they wanted was a bunch of preaching with a lot of hollering, screaming, running, singing, and dancing. Don't get me wrong, I do like to preach. And I like to run, and sing, and dance too. But sometimes, the anointing is in the teaching — in the expounding and explaining of something in the WORD. We first teach people who they are in Christ. Then, those people will live victoriously and be able to teach other people.

If someone gets healed and delivered, we thank God for it. But, if their mind hasn't been renewed by the WORD of God, eventually the devil will come back with a pain, or a symptom again. Then a thought will whisper, "Did you feel that? I thought God healed you? You must not have gotten healed after all." If they haven't been taught that they are truly healed, then they'll turn loose of their healing. On the other hand, if you teach somebody what God does for you in Jesus Christ, and they know how healing came by the WORD of God, and they know it belongs to them, then the devil can try all kinds of stuff and they'll say, "Oh no, this healing *is* mine. You just get out of here devil!" This same thing applies for every promise in the Bible – not just healing.

Jesus told Brother Hagin, "When I was there in Mark 6, they had no honor. I could only heal a few people with minor ailments: headaches, maybe a backache or something, no cancer, no disease, no leprosy. Nothing major – only a few minor ailments." But then He added, "The reason I went right back to teaching again was because faith cometh by hearing and hearing by the WORD of God[9]."

When we are teaching, preaching, and healing, I believe we are scripturally doing the works of Jesus. In our ministry, we stay close to the pattern Jesus set. For example, in meetings, I will usually always teach or preach before I call a healing line. Along the same lines, this book falls under the category of teaching, and I pray that it increases both your knowledge and your faith.

---

[9] Romans 10:17

Chapter 1 – Spirit, Soul, and Body

When you look at the course of a lifetime, my wife and I have been pastoring just a short time. But we started *serving* Jesus back in 1984 in the Ministry of Helps. Back then, we were door greeters, handed out the bulletins, taught Children's Church, and attended the parking lots. Anything our pastors needed help with, we were willing to do. In the short time that we've ministered and been around the things of God, one of the things I noticed is that a lot of times people get saved, and then almost immediately they are cut loose and told, in not so many words, "Now, you're saved and ready for Heaven. That's about it. You're on your own. Good luck!"

But God would not be a good father if all He did was make us ready for Heaven and then leave us for the wolves here on Planet Earth. Our Heavenly Father is not a dead-beat dad. No! He loves us so much He not only made provision for us once we leave Earth, but He also made provision for us while we are still here.

The Church ought to be the most victorious, healthiest, and richest bunch on the planet. God wants us to demonstrate to the world that He's a good father. The devil is a hard task-master, but not God. We're His kids. So if we're broke, busted, disgusted, sick, and depressed, then it's not God's fault. And, if that *is* going on, it isn't because we aren't saved or aren't His children. Many of us are even filled with Holy Ghost, speak in tongues, and flow in the gifts. So what's the problem then?

The problem is a lack of understanding about who we are in Christ, what's been made available to us, and exactly what gets made new (and what doesn't) at spiritual salvation. Consequently, we aren't demonstrating that we have a very good father taking care of us.

We must have knowledge about spiritual things because the devil always moves in ignorance. Ignorance doesn't mean lack of intelligence or the inability to learn. It means lack of knowledge. That's why Hosea, the prophet, recorded God as saying, *"My people are destroyed for a lack of knowledge..." (Hosea 4:6a, KJV)*. So if the devil moves in ignorance, then the more WORD of God we understand, the more we are able to prevent him from working in our lives.

Humans are Triune Beings

In this book we will be looking at the different aspects of the spirit, soul, and body. We are going to cover a lot of very familiar Scriptures. Even though you may know many of them by heart, it is important to look at them again with your eyes, read them aloud with your mouth, and hear them again with your ears. We want to study the Bible closely and go over these things again to establish a firm foundation to build upon.

So, let's begin at The Beginning:

> *26 And God said, **Let us make man in our image, after our likeness:** and let them have dominion over the fish of the sea, and over the fowl of the air, and over the cattle, and over all the earth, and over every creeping thing that creepeth upon the earth. (Genesis 1:26, KJV, emphasis added)*

13

Later, in John 4, when Jesus was talking to the woman at the well, He told her some very personal stuff about her own life. But, for our purposes, we want to look closely at what He told her in verse 24 about *what kind of being* God is.

> *24 **God is a Spirit**: and they that worship him must worship him in spirit and in truth. (John 4:24, KJV, emphasis added)*

So when you take these two verses together what do they tell us about what kind of beings we are? Well, in John 4:24 it says, "*God is a Spirit...*" Then from the very beginning, in Genesis 1:26, we are told that we are made in the image and likeness of God. So, this shows us we are spirits just like God. We're not just empty bodies walking around on this planet. We have a body; and, much like an astronaut has a spacesuit which makes it legal for him to operate in space, our body makes it legal for us to operate here on Earth. I like to call it our earthsuit as a reminder of its true purpose.

Now, let's take a closer look at the spirit and the soul.

> *12 For the word of God is quick, and powerful, and sharper than any two edged sword, piercing even to the **dividing asunder of soul and spirit**, and of the joints and marrow, and is a discerner of **the thoughts and intents of the heart**. (Hebrews 4:12, KJV, emphasis added)*

When we look closely at Hebrews 4:12, we see that the soul can be divided asunder[10] from your spirit. Therefore, it must be different than your spirit. If they were the same thing, you wouldn't be able to divide them. However, the two run so closely together that many times it takes revelation from the WORD of God to divide them and to show you how they are different.

---

[10] Asunder is an old English word that means "into parts" ("Asunder").

In the Bible, we often see the English word "heart". It never refers to the blood pump, and usually refers to the core being – the spirit man. However, occasionally we will see the English words "heart" and "soul" used interchangeably in Scripture. Hebrews 4:12 is one of those occasions. According to the original Greek, the phrase, "...*the thoughts and intents of the heart*," is referring to our will, the things we think about, our emotions, and our desires, but not our core spirit being (Strong's). Therefore, because they are not part of the spirit and they are not part of the physical body, we see that those things make up the soul. From this we can understand the WORD of God is a discerner of, "...*the thoughts and intents of the soul.*" So, when we put this all together, we now also understand that our soul is separate from our spirit and is made up of our mind, our will, and our emotions.

Let's take a look at what Apostle Paul wrote about how the spirit, soul, and body are interconnected.

> [23] *And the very God of peace sanctify you wholly; and* **I pray God your whole spirit and soul and body** *be preserved blameless unto the coming of our Lord Jesus Christ. (1 Thessalonians 5:23, KJV, emphasis added)*

Notice that Paul wrote, "*I pray God your whole spirit and soul and body...*" Remember, nothing in the Bible is an accident. He emphasizes these three parts separately and in a specific order because they *are separate but interconnected* entities within human beings. However, it is important to remember they have a proper order: spirit first, soul second, and then body last. You are a spirit – not a body – not a soul. Since you are made in the image and likeness of God, you are a spirit who possesses a soul and lives in a body. But always remember, the real you is a spirit.

Physical Death vs. Spiritual Death

On the sixth day, God made man to be the crown jewel of His creation and placed him in the Garden of Eden. Man was made in the image and likeness of God[11]. This means they were not only spirit beings like God, but they were also clothed in the same glory as God. That's why they had no need to cover their nakedness – they were already covered. Additionally, God gave man His dominion and authority over all of creation[12]. At that point in history, man enjoyed unhindered communion with each other and with God[13] (Of course we know that didn't last very long).

> [16] *And the* LORD *God commanded the man, saying, "Of every tree of the garden thou mayest freely eat:*
>
> [17] *But of the tree of the knowledge of good and evil, thou shalt not eat of it:* **for in the day that thou eatest thereof thou shalt surely die.** *"(Genesis 2:16-17, KJV, emphasis added)*

We see here in Genesis 2 that God told Adam they would die if they ate from the Tree of Knowledge of Good and Evil, and just a few verses over[14] we see they both did just that. Now I'm not a Hebrew expert, but from what I can tell, around 930 years *after* they partook from that tree Adam was still alive[15]. So, from this, we understand God wasn't referring to physical death in Genesis 2:17. But we also understand if you die spiritually, it will

---

[11] Genesis 1:26-31

[12] Genesis 1:26-2:16

[13] Genesis 2:25 and Genesis 3:8

[14] Genesis 3:6

[15] Genesis 5:5

eventually lead to your physical death. So at the time Adam partook of the fruit, he sinned and died spiritually.

Now, according to Romans 3:23, *"For all have sinned and fall short of the glory of God" (KJV).* So when Adam and Eve died spiritually, the light went out – the glory left them. Pretty quickly they recognized they had to get some other means of cover. They tried tying fig leaves around themselves, but the truth is they didn't just need a covering for their physical body. They needed redemption for the sin that had just infected their spirits. God, being the good Father that He is, made the first animal sacrifice that day to make clothes for them. It wasn't a permanent sacrifice to cleanse them from their sin. However, He did give them a promise that in the future One would come who would crush the serpent under foot and restore everything they had just given away to Satan in that act of high treason[16].

Changed in the Twinkling of an Eye – The Perishable Body

Remember in I Thessalonians 5:23 Paul said, *"...I pray God your whole spirit and soul and body be preserved blameless unto the coming of our Lord Jesus Christ" (KJV).* A lot of Christians say, "Well, I'm saved, that's all I've got to do." But right here Paul is telling us there is more to this. People often misunderstand this prayer. Paul is not praying that God will do this *for* the believer. He is praying to God that *the believer will be faithful to keep his soul and body blameless* until the coming of Jesus. In other words, that they will keep renewing their minds daily, walking the life of faith daily, and enduring through every circumstance daily – never giving up.

---

[16] Genesis 3:15

The body we currently have cannot go to Heaven the way it is. Even if we are alive and remain until the coming of Jesus, the Bible tells us two things will happen. First, according to I Thessalonians 4:15, we will not go ahead of those who have died. They shall come with the LORD. And then, second, when the rapture (or the catching away of the church) comes, then we who are alive and remain, "....*shall be changed in a moment and a twinkling of an eye...*" (*I Corinthians 15:52, KJV*).

So what part of you will be changed in the twinkling of an eye? That will be the body. But, here's the important part to understand in all this, if your *spirit* wasn't already saved, then you're not going in the rapture. Do you understand? If you're not saved spiritually when the rapture happens, then there will be no bodily change for you. It's too late at that point. So, the important change that needs to take place, to prepare you to go in the rapture, happens when you were saved by grace and made new in your spirit.

Let me repeat that. The change that will happen at the rapture cannot be our spirit man, because our spirit man was already made brand new and rapture-ready at spiritual salvation[17]. From this then, we understand that God does not intend for the body of flesh to be the true man or to lead us, because it is designed for us to leave behind on this planet when we leave here either by physical death or by the rapture of the Church.

---

[17] If you aren't sure if you've experienced spiritual salvation, turn to Appendix 1 to learn more.

Lazarus and the Rich Man - A Discussion of the Soul

In Luke 16:19-31, Jesus gives us a beautiful picture of the permanency of the human spirit and soul, as well as, the stark difference that awaits those who accept God's gift of salvation and those who do not.

19 There was a certain rich man, which was clothed in purple and fine linen, and fared sumptuously every day:

20 And there was a certain beggar named Lazarus, which was laid at his gate, full of sores,

21 And desiring to be fed with the crumbs which fell from the rich man's table: moreover the dogs came and licked his sores.

22 And it came to pass, that the beggar died, and was carried by the angels into Abraham's bosom: the rich man also died, and was buried;

23 And in hell he lift up his eyes, being in torments, and seeth Abraham afar off, and Lazarus in his bosom.

24 And he cried and said, Father Abraham, have mercy on me, and send Lazarus, that he may dip the tip of his finger in water, and cool my tongue; for I am tormented in this flame.

25 But Abraham said, Son, remember that thou in thy lifetime receivedst thy good things, and likewise Lazarus evil things: but now he is comforted, and thou art tormented.

26 And beside all this, between us and you there is a great gulf fixed: so that they which would pass from hence to you cannot; neither can they pass to us, that would come from thence.

27 Then he said, I pray thee therefore, father, that thou wouldest send him to my father's house:

28 For I have five brethren; that he may testify unto them, lest they also come into this place of torment.

29 Abraham saith unto him, They have Moses and the prophets; let them hear them.

30 And he said, Nay, father Abraham: but if one went unto them from the dead, they will repent.

31 And he said unto him, If they hear not Moses and the prophets, neither will they be persuaded, though one rose from the dead. (Luke 16:19-31, KJV)

Before Jesus died and rose from the dead, the saints of old were only cleansed in the flesh through the sacrifices. Their sin was only covered through the sacrifice of animals. Colossians 1:18 tells us Jesus was the first begotten from the dead. Nobody was spiritually alive – that took the Blood of Jesus for you and me.

So there was a holding tank of sorts, called Paradise or Abraham's Bosom. It was down in the earth by hell. However, it was not in hell, because there was this great gulf separating the two. It is important to understand, since Jesus died and rose again, that place has been shut down. Now, when anyone who believes in Him leaves their earthsuit, they go straight to Heaven. We no longer go to Abraham's Bosom. We go straight into the very presence of God[18].

---

[18] 2 Corinthians 5:8

We can tell from verse 27 that this rich man is in hell. He is in the place of torment. His body is in the grave back on the surface of Planet Earth and his spirit and soul are in hell being tormented. Notice that he recognizes Lazarus and Abraham. He talks about Lazarus' finger and his own tongue. Yet we know both of these men are dead and their bodies are in the grave starting to stink. This shows us that our spirit man looks just like our physical man.

Now, let's turn our discussion to the soul. His brain is an organ. So, just like his blood pumping heart, we know his brain is in the grave with the rest of his body. Yet here he is remembering and talking about his kinfolk back home. This shows us that our soul cannot simply be the result of the functioning brain. Our mind, our will, and our emotions are separate from, and far more than, our brain.

Because of this, Christians should never say things like, "I'm just losing my mind," or "That just blows my mind," or "My memory's fading fast!" Your mind is in your soul. Now, if you've got problems with your brain, we can get that healed, but we can't heal your soul – you have to renew it with the WORD of God. The important point I want you to see here is that your spirit and soul are both eternal, while your body is not.

Chapter 2 – The Importance of Transforming the Soul

Made to Crave

As Christians, we are confident that any person who asks Jesus into his heart (meaning the spirit not the blood pump) and believes Jesus died and rose again, becomes a new creature in Christ Jesus[19]. In our Christian vernacular, we say that person is born again. But we need to understand exactly what being made a new creature or being born again means.

> *[17] Therefore **if any man be in Christ**, he is a new creature: old things are passed away; behold, all things are become new. (2 Corinthians 5:17, KJV, emphasis added)*

As I was meditating on this, the LORD began to talk to me about things in the area of the soul and He said, "If you'll notice, the same soul they had before they got saved is the exact same soul they had after they got saved. The spirit of a man is the only part of them that became brand new at the new birth."

So, let's look at 2 Corinthians 5:17 very closely to understand what He means. Where does it say we become brand new? It says that, "*...if any man be in Christ...*" Therefore, since Christ is no longer walking this Earth, the only way you and I can be in Christ is to join with Him spiritually. That happened the day you and I asked Jesus into our lives. On that day, we were made brand new in our spirit man and only in our spirit man.

---

[19] See also Romans 10:9-10

To put it another way, when we get saved, it's easy for us to see that the body – the outward man – didn't become brand new. If you are brown-headed right before you asked Jesus into your heart, you will still be brown-headed after. But was the soul, which is made up of the mind, the will, and the emotions, saved or made brand new and set apart for Christ at that same time? No. It was not. And that is not so easy for us to see with our eyes. Just like with hair color, if you liked to gossip before asking Jesus into your life, you're still going to like to gossip when you walk away from that prayer. This is true because saving the soul, or changing the way we think and behave to line up with God's ways, is not instantaneous. It is a process that takes an investment of time.

Apostle Paul wrote the book of Romans to the Church at Rome, and also to you and I, to help us all understand this process.

> [1] *I beseech you therefore, brethren, by the mercies of God, that ye present your bodies a living sacrifice, holy, acceptable unto God, which is your reasonable service.*
>
> [2] *And be not conformed to this world: but **be ye transformed by the renewing of your mind**, that ye may prove what is that **good**, and **acceptable**, and **perfect**, will of God. (Romans 12:1-2, KJV, emphasis added)*

Look again at Romans 12:2, Paul wrote, "*...be not conformed to this world...*" The Earth is the LORD's and the fullness thereof[20]. But the world's *systems* are influenced by the devil because he is the god of this world[21]. The word "conform" means to fashion or shape one thing just like another. Isn't it

---

[20] Psalm 24:1

[21] 2 Corinthians 4:4

amazing, Paul wasn't writing to unsaved folks? He was writing to a group of Christians at Rome. He's writing to the Church! They're all born again and spiritually alive unto God. Their newly reborn spirits are alive unto God, and yet he writes, "Don't be conformed to think like the spirit that is influencing the world." Why did he write that? Because he knew if they conformed to the world in their personal lives, eventually they would allow the spirit of the world to come into the Church. Through Paul's writing, God is still telling us today, don't be conformed to think like, or operate by, the same spirit that influences the world. Instead be transformed by the renewing of your mind with the WORD.

So, according to Scripture, this is why born-again Christians who don't renew their minds with the WORD of God have so much trouble and struggle with sin in their lives – even if they are Spirit-filled and pray in tongues. They have a brand new spirit made to crave after the things of God, but they have the same old thoughts, emotions, and self-will craving after the things of the world. Every day is a tug-of-war.

Brand New Versus Renewed

As soon as someone believes that Jesus is the Son of God, that He died and rose again as a substitute and sacrifice for them, and they ask Him into their life as their Savior, they become alive to God. Instantly they receive a brand new spirit[22]. Let me share an example that will help illustrate what happens to the soul:

We used to have an old rocker that my wife, Pastor Sally, used to rock all our kids. The arms weren't wooden, but it had some wood in the front where all the kids had chewed on it when

---

[22] 2 Corinthians 5:21, Romans 10:9-10 & 13, and 2 Corinthians 5:17

they were cutting their teeth. It meant a lot to my wife because all those little teeth marks reminded her of when they were babies. So we kept it and carried it with us every time we moved. Eventually, after we moved to Pawnee from Silsbee, we ended up putting it out on the back porch. She just never wanted to throw it away because it brought too many sweet memories. It sat out there for years and years until the material and stuffing was bad.

One day, she came to me and said, "Hon, I want to have that old rocking chair reupholstered."

So, we took it down to a local upholstery shop and the guy was very honest with us. He told us up front, "It will cost you about three times more to get it reupholstered than what a brand new one would cost."

I replied, "I realize that, and I appreciate you being so honest with us. But we want this one because it has sentimental value. I'd like you to just put it back as good as you can and make it look new."

So, he put new brass buttons on it and a new foam seat where the old coil springs had been broken. He did several different things and then he covered it with new cloth. He made it look good and then we took it home. It looked so good, in fact, that almost as soon as we got it home our daughter took it!

Now, imagine the person that bought that chair in the beginning. When they picked it up, it wasn't *renewed* it was *brand new*. It was all wrapped up in plastic wrap and maybe in a cardboard box to protect it. That's what happened to you and me when we got saved spiritually. We were given brand new spirits. We're as saved as we can be when we ask Jesus into our hearts. We are ready for Heaven. We are born again. We are children of God – and we are just like our Father.

But, like that old rocker left neglected on the back porch, if our soul never gets renewed or saved with the WORD of God, it will fight us. A reupholstered rocker isn't brand new. It has been made over from the inside out. That's what we want for our will, our mind, and our emotions. We want them transformed from the inside out so they will agree with our spirit man. We can see from this simple natural example a powerful spiritual principle: *we are looking to get our soul renewed.* Say this out loud, "I'm after a renewed soul."

People who are unsure if they truly got saved are usually confused on this concept. Often, they make a confession of faith and they expect everything in their life to change automatically. They expect to get up from that prayer and every bad habit or thought in their life will be gone without them having to do anything. But when that isn't the case, they'll say, "Maybe I didn't get saved?" If they made a confession of faith in Jesus and really meant it, then they did! They probably just need to spend some more time renewing their mind with the WORD of God so their soul can catch up to their spirit and begin agreeing with it.

2/3 Majority Wins!

I have a saying to help people remember how the spirit-soul-body connection works, "Two-thirds majority wins!" Because, when you have two against one, the third part has no choice but to follow along. Your born again spirit is made to crave after the things of God and will always agree with God's will. Therefore, we always want our spirit man to lead and our soul to line up and agree with it. That leaves the flesh with no other option but to follow. Otherwise, when your spirit is saved but your soul isn't, your soul will join forces with your flesh and you will have a struggle! As a result, the enemy walks right in and has a heyday in your life.

An unrenewed mind will continue to think and operate according to the influence of the world. That's why sometimes you'll see a person do certain things and you think, "I'm not sure he's really saved." Well, probably what's happened is that his soul hasn't been saved even though he made a true confession of faith in Jesus. His spirit got saved, but because the soul isn't automatically saved, he continues to have the same thoughts, emotions, words, and actions that he had before he got spiritually saved because his soul and flesh are dominating his spirit. However, over time, as this same Christian begins to study the WORD of God and renew his mind, things will start to change as his soul begins to line up with his spirit. At that point, he will be able to more easily control his flesh and the way he behaves.

Here's an example from my own life:

In the Body of Christ, there are several denominations that don't mind if ministers drink. One day, there was one guy teasing me because I don't drink. So I explained to him, "Well, Sir, I used to drink like a fish." It's true! There are eight years of my life that are gone. I don't know where I was or what I did. Except I know I was in and out of jail and everything else that goes with that kind of lifestyle.

You see, I didn't care about social drinking, because I wasn't sociable. I drank to get drunk – slobbering, falling down drunk was always my motive. After a while, beer alone wouldn't do that anymore. So I turned to whiskey. When it quit working, I turned to pills, then marijuana, and all that other stuff you lace it with. My goal was always to get higher than a Georgia Pine.

So, I told him, "I used to drink, and once I got saved I still tried to for a while. But, something in my heart kept scratching at me. I wondered what it was. So, I got to digging around in the Scripture and began renewing my mind on the subject. When I did that, God showed me why I drank. Do you know the reason I wanted to drink?"

"No Sir."

"So I would feel better. Then, when I got filled with the Holy Ghost, suddenly I realized I didn't have to be filled with something else to feel better. The WORD changed my mind and I quit drinking."

Just because I kept drinking for a while doesn't mean I wasn't saved. My confession of faith in Jesus is what saved me – not whether I quit drinking or not. But, I wanted to live the victorious life here and now on Earth. So I renewed my mind and got God's opinion on the subject and quit. 2/3 majority wins! Those habits literally melted away as I began to replace my way of thinking with God's thoughts from His WORD. See, once I got drunk on the Holy Ghost and start living the good life with Jesus, I had no desire to go back to that old life.

When I tell stories about my old life, a lot of Christians say, "Well that's wonderful what God did for you. But I've never struggled with drugs or alcohol and I don't smoke." They just can't relate to that hard living. But a lot of Christians that don't smoke or drink worry, which is also a sin (and it shortens lives too by the way). It doesn't matter what the sin habit is, people usually say the same thing, "Oh man, my heart…" In other words, down in their spirit where the life of God is, they recognize they don't really want to do it, but it has a hold of their flesh. Therefore, once they get a revelation of the life of God that's on the inside of them, it begins to melt away those habits and change their behaviors. But no matter what, always remember, drinking, smoking, cussing, worrying, and overeating stuff isn't going to send anyone to hell. The only thing that will stop you from going to Heaven is not having Jesus in your life. So never condemn someone that is still struggling with a sin habit, because faith works by love[23].

---

[23] Galatians 5:6

Chapter 3 – Renew Your Mind and Comb Your Hair Daily

Transforming Cars and Ships on the Sea

My grandkids love the movie *Transformers*[24] and in it there is a yellow Camaro named Bumble Bee. He'll be driving along and then, all of a sudden, he starts to change – to transform. Suddenly he stands up ready to do battle. What does he transform into? A warrior – a fighting machine. Spiritually speaking, that's what happens when you and I renew our mind with the WORD on a daily basis. We begin to transform into Bible-toting, devil-stomping, diligent, and anointed Christians.

Therefore, if you don't transform your mind, you're not really going to be in a position to do anything with the devil. Eventually the devil will come along and say, "You know what? You're not going to make it. You're sick. You're going to die of it." Or, "You're broke. You're not going to ever get out of debt…da-da-da…" He's going to whip you in your mind, because that's the arena he moves in. But when you have renewed your mind with the WORD of God, it will come up and out of you and suddenly you've transformed into a warrior right before his very eyes. And that warrior in you will shout, "Oh devil, you're a liar. You are under my feet in the name of Jesus!"

---

[24] *Transformers* is a live-action movie released by DreamWorks in 2007, with Executive Producer Steven Spielberg and Director Michael Bay.

By now we are starting to understand why we'll see some Christians who never seem to get victory. They seem to always be riding a roller coaster up one day and down the next, in church this week and out of church the next. Even though their spirit is saved, their soul is trying to conform to the world rather than transforming into a soldier in God's army.

> *23 And be renewed **in the spirit of your mind;***
>
> *24 And that ye **put on the new man**, which after God is created in righteousness and true holiness. (Ephesians 4:25-29, KJV, emphasis added)*

In Ephesians, Apostle Paul is writing to the Christians at Ephesus (and to you and me). In verse 23, the phrase, *"...in the spirit of your mind,"* is referring to the soul – the mind, the will, and the emotions. In some older King James Versions you'll see the word "nature" instead of "man" in verse 24. What does Paul mean by this? The new man or new nature is talking about your newly reborn spirit man. So, Paul is saying that a person who's soul never got saved will still be dominated under the influence of the world even though they're saved and their spirit man is wanting to do right.

Let me give you another helpful illustration. Think of a ship controlled by a captain at the helm (the big steering wheel in the center of the ship). We want our ship to be controlled by our spirit so it will go only in the direction God wants us to go. But if your soul is *also* trying to lead at the helm of your life, your boat isn't going to go very far. Either your soul will steer you in the complete opposite direction of God, or your spirit will pull the helm one way and your soul will pull it the opposite. In that case, your forward momentum will pretty much stall out. Hence the reason Paul instructs us to put on the new man. You can only have one captain driving the boat if you expect to get anywhere. This is especially true if you want to get where God wants you to go.

Renew Your Mind to Get Into the Perfect Will of God

Brother Kenneth E. Hagin put it this way, "Your mind will not stay renewed any more than your hair will stay combed." You have to comb your hair every day. It is the same with our soul. Therefore, we must renew our mind every day with the WORD of God because only God's WORD has the power to transform us from the inside out. It is the revealed will of God. So, when we are reading the WORD, we don't have to be guessing about God's will. We can actually, *"...prove what is that good, and acceptable, and perfect, will of God" (Romans 12:2, KJV).*

Did you catch that? There are actually three wills of God: Good, Acceptable, and Perfect. What keeps Christians out of the perfect will of God is our soul or our thinking. That's why people will fight you concerning prosperity, health, victory, and complete deliverance. You see, without a renewed mind, people will think God doesn't want them to be prosperous. Without a renewed mind, people will think God wants some people to die sick. But aren't you glad the will of God is that everybody will be well? Jesus bore stripes for everybody[25]. But, you have to understand, it takes a renewed mind to get that prosperity or that healing. It takes a renewed mind to prove the perfect will of God according to the WORD of God. Let me show you an example of an area where I had to renew my mind.

The writer of Hebrews says, *"And as it is appointed unto men once to die, but after this the judgment" (Hebrews 9:27, KJV).*

---

[25] Isaiah 53:5 and 1 Peter 2:24

What part of man is that referring to? Well, it's obvious that it can only be referring to the physical part or the body. Years ago I was taught that this meant we had an *appointed time to die* and that was it – when your *time* was up it was up.

But then I was taught about Proverbs 3:1-3, and it says that if we don't forget God and keep His commandments they will *add* length of days and long life to you. Well, if you had an appointed time to die, then it wouldn't matter how you lived, good or bad, when your appointed time came you'd die – there would be no way to *add* length to your days.

Here's the deal, Hebrews 9:27 doesn't say we have an appointed *time* to die, it says we are going to die *once* which is supposed to be *when you are finished*. We know this because in Paul's letter to the Philippians he wrote, *"For I am in a strait betwixt two, having a desire to depart, and to be with Christ; which is far better. Nevertheless to abide in the flesh is more needful for you" (Philippians 1:23-24, KJV).* Paul chose when he left.

In Ephesians 6:1, children are told to obey their parents in the Lord, and to honor their fathers and mothers, so that they will live long on the Earth. If I'm not supposed to live a long time, then we might as well rip that page right out of the Bible. So often, what happens is people will get saved and they'll join a church, but then they never renew their mind with the WORD to get their soul saved. So, they're still out drinking, carousing, running around, carrying on, and all that stuff. Then something bad happens and they die young. When that happens, people start saying, "Well, see, they had an appointed time to die." No, they didn't, they were just ignorant of the devil's devices. He short-circuited their life and God's plan for their life. I don't mean to be cruel, but it's the truth.

It took quite a lot of studying the WORD of God for me to see the danger in this "appointed time" doctrine. If a person thinks he has an appointed time to die then he will naturally begin to set that time in his own mind – usually based on when others in his family tended to die. Then if a sickness or something tries to attack his body around that age he will have no reason to fight to stay alive or to use his faith to believe for healing. You can even see it before someone gets sick. When they believe this doctrine and are nearing that time in their mind, they will stop using their faith to walk in the divine health that Jesus provided for them because they're just turning everything over. They're sort of saying, "Well, God it's up to you now." But really, God has left it up to us.

First Graders Don't Know How to Do Algebra

Ephesians 4:24 reminds us that we've been made the righteousness of God in Christ Jesus. You can't get any more right with God than that. I'm talking about in your spirit. But the revelation about how a righteous person *lives* can grow. The same way a first grader doesn't know how to do Algebra, but eventually learns as he grows and gets educated, is the same way a Christian learns about how to live righteously.

Now, let's read a little further:

> 25 Wherefore putting away lying, speak every man truth with his neighbour: for we are members one of another.
>
> 26 Be ye angry, and sin not: let not the sun go down upon your wrath:
>
> 27 Neither give place to the devil.
>
> 28 Let him that stole steal no more: but rather let him labour, working with his

hands the thing which is good, that he may have to give to him that needeth.

29 Let no corrupt communication proceed out of your mouth, but that which is good to the use of edifying, that it may minister grace unto the hearers. (Ephesians 4:25-29, KJV)

In verses 25-28 of Ephesians 4, Paul admonishes Christians about lying and anger, because, according to verse 27, anger gives the devil a foothold that he can exploit in your soul and flesh. This means if you are ticked off at somebody, make sure you don't go to bed holding a grudge. It'll mess with you and hurt you.

You know, I used to do that. I would get angry and hold out. I would stay angry at Sally all day. Then, right before sunset, I'd say, "Please forgive me." I was trying to be scriptural because I knew it was not good to go to bed mad at anyone – especially for husbands and wives. But that's all I understood at the time. Eventually, as I renewed my mind, I learned it was a whole lot better to deal with that issue sooner rather than later so my whole day wasn't ruined. I began to grow and mature in my understanding of righteousness and how a righteous person lives.

As we read on through Ephesians 4:28 and 29, we see Paul reminding these same Christians to stop stealing and to clean up their language. More often than not, we forget that he wrote this letter to the *Church*. It would be just like me writing a letter to one of the churches where I minister and reminding them of these things. These were real problems for them back then, and they are still problems for us today when we don't renew our minds to think and operate God's way.

When I teach on this subject, I always get people who will bristle somewhat. They'll say things along the lines of, "Well, Brother Ricky, I'm just not a put-on. I'm just real."

My response to that is always, "Yeah? You're real? Real carnal." Carnality[26] is a real issue – even in the church. We need to understand it if we are going to get victory over it.

Carnality Opens the Door to Oppression

When I was growing up in the Assemblies of God, I thought everyone in the church was a saint. My siblings and I never heard our parents discuss any of the church members at the house. As far as I know, they never discussed any problem with the family, the church, or anyone else, for that matter, before us kids. They didn't believe in gossip.

But as I got older, I started noticing things. I remember some of the deacons were having some problems and difficulties. Some were mad at each other and different things. As I noticed these things, I became confused because I had heard some of these men give a message in tongues, or interpret, or praise God. But then later, I would see them having "fits of carnality" which caused me to wonder if they were really saved. The truth is they were just as saved as you can get, because anybody who asks Jesus into their heart is born again. They might have been carnal, but they were born again.

Similarly, a person once said to me, "Well, I won't go to church because all the hypocrites are there."

---

[26] The word "carnal" comes from a Latin word referring to the flesh, or body. But, even more specifically, it is referring to the passions, appetites, and desires of the flesh. Carnality also refers to things of the world as opposed to things of the spirit (Carnal).

I thought to myself, "That's like saying I won't go to the Emergency Room because of all the sick people there." Well, that's why it's there. We don't go to church because people are perfect. We go because we want to hang out with God and with His folk. We love the family of God. The church family loves God and gathers around Jesus and the WORD. We're all learning and growing in certain areas of our lives.

Along these same lines, one guy told me, "Well you don't have to go to church to be saved."

I replied, "Dear God, anybody with any sense at all ought to know that. All you have to do to be saved is ask Jesus into your heart." But, salvation alone won't make you victorious. You can be a Christian and be just as carnal as somebody who goes to the beer joint every night. You can have cussing fits and ask everybody to forgive you, and they will. You can be all carnal and start running folk off the road in traffic. You can. You naturally have a right to because you have a human body and a free will, but do you have a moral right to do it? If you keep doing stuff like that, eventually people are going to start saying, "If he's a Christian, why would I want to be like him?" Remember, just because you have human right to do something, doesn't make it right.

We don't want to see how close to sin we can get and still make Heaven. We're out to live holy lives. We want to be different because we are called the Light of the World[27]. Therefore, we want to study this subject of carnal Christianity carefully so we can have victory and live like the blessed people we are. You can get saved and never change your behavior one iota. You can be a Christian and be just as carnal as everyone else in the world dealing with all

---

[27] Matthew 5:14-16

the same struggles if you want. You can. You have a free will. But, you'll live a defeated life if you do.

So let's look at an example of what I'm talking about. James, The LORD's half-brother by his mother Mary, was a pastor in Jerusalem. He wrote to an interesting group of Christians. Read James 1:21, but pay particular attention to the last phrase.

> *21 Wherefore lay apart all filthiness and superfluity of naughtiness, and receive with **meekness**[28] the engrafted word, **which is able to save your souls.** (James 1:21, KJV, emphasis added)*

Basically, James wrote to these Christians and told them that their souls were not saved. This was a bunch of church people who loved Jesus. But, from the looks of it, they were dealing with some very serious problems of the soulish realm. There's no doubt that they were born again spiritually and on their way to Heaven. Yet their minds, wills, and emotions hadn't been saved and set apart for Christ. That's what held them in that arena of filthiness[29] and superfluity[30] of naughtiness[31]. People whose emotions run a roller coaster have unsaved souls. In other words, they haven't changed their minds about those things.

---

[28] Meekness means a quiet and humble spirit. It does not mean weakness or that you won't stand up for what is right.

[29] Definition of Filthiness: very dirty; very offensive or disgusting and usually about sex; very evil; morally wrong (Merriam-Webster)

[30] Definition of Superfluity: *1a*: excess, oversupply *1b*: something unnecessary or superfluous *2*: immoderate and especially luxurious living, habits, or desires (Merriam-Webster)

[31] Definition of Naughtiness: behaving badly; relating to or suggesting sex in usually a playful way (Merriam-Webster)

Let's dig a little deeper into Romans 12:2 to understand this better.

> 2 *And be not conformed to this world:* *but **be ye transformed by the renewing** **of your mind**, that ye may prove what is that good, and acceptable, and perfect, will of God. (Romans 12:2, KJV, emphasis added)*

In Romans 12:2, Paul tells us, *"...be not conformed to this world; but be ye transformed by the renewing of your mind..."* Now, if you are like me, it can be a job to get your mind renewed. I grew up thinking it was wrong to have money – I'm not exactly sure why – I just did. I didn't know where it was in the Bible, but I could quote, *"It is easier for a camel to go through the eye of a needle than for a rich man to get into heaven" (Mark 10:25, KJV).* I thought they were talking about trying to get a full grown animal through one of those little sewing needles. God's not opposed to Christians being rich. God's not opposed to Christians being well. But you have to know, there is God's way to go about it and then there is the world's way.

If you have a journal or a notebook you use for taking notes, write down this definition of a carnal Christian:

> *Even though Christians are saved, born again, and Spirit-filled, if their minds are not renewed and developed by the WORD, their soul will side with the flesh; and the devil, through the flesh, will dominate them.*

Our flesh is not saved. So when your soul isn't saved either, you'll find yourself thinking things like:

- "You hit me — I'll hit you."
- "You talk about me — I'll talk about you."

- "I can act this way if I want to."

- "It's my party and I'll cry if I want to..." as the old song goes[32].

Look at that definition of a carnal Christian again. Now, focus on the words, *"...and the devil, through the flesh, will dominate them."* It is important to understand that demons cannot live in the born again spirit because the Holy Spirit lives there, and according to 1 John 4:4, *"Greater is He that is in you than he that is in the world" (KJV).* The devil is in the world – outside the believer's spirit.

But, according to Acts 10:38, demons oppress and harass both the body and the soul of a believer.

> [38] *How God anointed Jesus of Nazareth with the Holy Ghost and with power: who went about doing good, and healing all that were **oppressed of the devil**; for God was with him. (Acts 10:38, KJV, emphasis added)*

Focus on the phrase, *"...oppressed of the devil..."* All sickness and all disease is satanic oppression and harassment to be sure. In Luke 10:13-17 we find the story of the woman with the *spirit of infirmity* that had been bent over for 18 years and could not raise herself. She had an actual demon attached to her causing her infirmity.

But this is not always the case. Remember in John 9, the disciples asked Jesus, *"Rabbi, why was this man born blind? Was it because of his own sins or his parents' sins?" (John 9:1, NKJV).* He answered them that neither had sinned. In other words this

---

[32] "It's My Party" by Leslie Gore

illness was not caused by a demon hanging on to a foothold such as anger or worry. This illness was present from birth.

We know from Romans 5:12 that the death to this man's vision didn't come from God and God didn't give permission for it either. It was a work of the devil. What are the works of the devil? Death, sickness, poverty, lack, etc. They are the things found in the curse of Deuteronomy 28:15-68. Furthermore, we understand from 1 John 3:8-9 that Jesus came to destroy the works of the devil. So, on this day, Jesus was not only going to heal this man's blindness, but He was also going to make a show of God's power[33] to crush the works of the devil.

The devil can only oppress, or dominate, someone if their soul has not been saved, and if they are thinking with an unrenewed mind. This is because an unrenewed mind gives demons plenty of footholds, such as anger[34], to climb up and hang on like a 50-lb backpack. This weighs the believer down and limits his movements, but the demon never has complete control of the believer. However, when the soul has been saved, it thinks like God, no longer chases after the things of the world, and provides no footholds for the devil to exploit. In the case of the man born blind, though a demon was not continuously causing his illness, he still had the responsibility to renew his mind to God's will to heal him and to participate in his healing by washing in the pool of Siloam when instructed by Jesus. If he had failed to do either, he most likely would not be listed in the Bible today.

---

[33] John 9:1-12

[34] Ephesians 4:26

A Broken Church Set Free

Baby Christians aren't the only ones to struggle with unrenewed minds. Sometimes, mature, godly men and women can be blinded to areas that need to be renewed in their own souls.

A few years back, there was a pastor at an Assembly of God church. I happened to be preaching at another place and some of his people showed up at my meeting and asked, "Oh my, would you please come to our church?"

I answered, "I'll go wherever the LORD tells me to go."

"Well, if our pastor calls you, will you come?" they persisted.

Again, I answered, "I'll go anywhere the LORD says to go." Sure enough, that pastor called a little later and the LORD said for me to go. So, I went. Come to find out, he had cancer and his wife was deaf in her left ear.

Now, this church was a big straight building with two big sections of seating and a row down the middle. The first night, there was one deacon on the right about five rows back, and two older deacons were sitting on the other side about halfway back on the outside aisle. That night, as I was teaching on 1 Corinthians 11, the deacon sitting on the right spoke right up smack in the middle of my sermon and said, "Well, that ain't right! I don't believe a word of it."

He said this out loud, and it's a good thing my soul was saved, because my flesh wanted to do something. So, I went a little further in my message and one of the deacons on the other side spoke up and said some stuff too. My goodness was it a struggle! I even called my wife and told her to call my ministry partners and tell them pray because we were having such a struggle there the first two or three days. Each night, I would ask the LORD about this situation and seek His guidance.

It turned out there was an elderly lady in the crowd who had been an evangelist in the Assemblies of God. Every night after the sermon, she would stand up and say, "This is God. It's right. It is what we used to listen to. It's in the Bible. He proved it all. Now you all straighten up."

I'm serious! I had my own cheering section! Glory to God! Halfway through my stay, she came up to me at the end of the meeting like she wanted to tell me something about those deacons. But I had to tell her, "Now don't tell me anything. I don't want to know anything," because I wanted to be free to say whatever The LORD led me to say without interference.

Finally, after we were all finished, she came back and asked me, "Can I tell you now?" At that point I agreed. She went on to ask, "Do you know why you struggled so?"

I answered, "Yes, I think so. But why don't you tell me."

So she explained, "Did you notice that this group, when you told everyone to shake hands, didn't shake hands with that group? And that group didn't shake hands with the other group? It's because they got mad over a certain thing the church wanted to do cosmetic-wise. And, since they didn't get their way, they got mad at this side over here. Now those are deacons I'm talking about."

Since these are deacons she's telling me about, we know they are born again. Some of them would quake and shake under the power and pray in tongues. But, then, they wouldn't talk with their brother sitting in the same building. They were saved and they were born again, but their souls were not. So their pastor had to deal with all of this and under the burden and pressure of it all, he developed cancer.

Each night, he'd sit there and, as God used me to say certain things, I would see his face change. He'd look at his wife and nod his head. When I saw him doing that, I thought along the lines of that old rock song, "Yep...another one bites the dust! And another one gone, and another one down...[35]" You know the Holy Ghost was just nailing him. Pow! Pow! Pow!

He was like, "Wow! This is good!" Soon enough, he was getting up at the end of the sermon saying, "Whew!! This is good folks!"

In a tongue-in-cheek sort of way, I was thinking, "Yeah, uh huh, you're letting me say all that with the help of the Holy Ghost." But it was all good. I could tell God was doing a mighty work.

We were there three or four nights. On the next to the last night, the pastor got a call that he needed to go back to M.D. Anderson Cancer Treatment Center in Galveston. He told me he was going to miss church that night. However, before he left, he said, "I'm going to be over there for all these tests. It's going to be a very long day. But I want you to know, just go ahead and keep doing what you've been doing. It's been wonderful."

Well, the next night when he came back he brought a report from the doctors. He was totally healed. He was completely cancer free. Not only was he healed, but his wife had also received total healing. She shouted and screamed and ran all over everywhere. Now as we were hearing these praise reports, the deacon over there

---

[35] "Another One Bites the Dust" by Queen

on the right (the one that didn't believe anything I said) stood up and declared, "I didn't like what was going on or agree with it. But you cannot deny the power of God." Glory to God!

In that short time God had me minister there, the pastor got totally healed, his wife got totally healed, and several others were healed too. The WORD of God was demonstrated by the power of God. It reminds me of a story about Elijah that I love. When Elijah was up on Mt. Carmel and he said to the prophets of Baal, "Let the God of power answer by fire[36]." Our God's alive! We're not talking about a dead religion. We're talking about a living God who loves us. This is why God wants us to know the Bible deeply. There are so many people out there that think God doesn't love them, or that He's put something on them to hurt them. When we know what the WORD says, then we've got the answer — God ain't mad at nobody. No, God's for humanity not against them. It's the devil who wants to kill humanity. God loves us.

I shared this story to show you that it isn't just unsaved folks that struggle with keeping their minds renewed and their soul saved. Some of those people in that church had been there over 50 years. They served God, loved God, loved the LORD Jesus, loved the WORD, and loved *almost* everybody they went to church with. But the sad part of it was that people in the world act exactly the same way. So, we see, they had never been completely transformed, because they were still conformed to the world even though they lived as children of God.

---

[36] 1 Kings 18:24

Chapter 4 – The Soul — Satan's Favorite Arena

The god of This World

The true temptations of Jesus are recorded in the book of Luke. It's important to remember that these events would not be called temptations if they were just some little annoyance Jesus had to deal with. In fact, Luke's account of the temptation of Jesus shows us very clearly why Christians should get their mind renewed with the WORD of God. Jesus shows us the proper pattern for dealing with temptation. But these verses also prove some very important points about the world. Let's study them carefully:

> *5 And the devil, taking him up into an high mountain, shewed unto him all the kingdoms of the world in a moment of time.*
>
> *6 And the devil said unto him, All this power will I give thee, and the glory of them: for that is delivered unto me; and to whomsoever I will I give it.*
>
> *7 If thou therefore wilt worship me, all shall be thine.*
>
> *8 And Jesus answered and said unto him, Get thee behind me, Satan: for it is written, Thou shalt worship the Lord thy God, and him only shalt thou serve. (Luke 4:5-8, KJV)*

In verse five, the devil is showing Jesus all the kingdoms of the world. Then, in verse six, the Bible says, *"And the devil said unto him, all this power will I give thee, and the glory of them: for that is delivered unto me; and to whomsoever I will I give it."* To put verse six into modern language it would go along the lines of, "I have control of all this. It's been turned over to me, and I can give it to anybody I want."

Did you catch what the devil just said? He said *all the kingdoms* in the world belonged to him. Is that true? Well, if it was not true, Jesus would have challenged him and said, "Devil, they're not yours to give." But we can see in verse eight that Jesus did not dispute what was said. Furthermore, if it wasn't true, this would not have been a true temptation for Jesus. Therefore they probably would not have even been recorded here. In addition, we know the devil got those worlds from Adam. The Bible clearly says, unlike Eve, Adam was not tricked into sinning – he consciously chose to eat that fruit[37]. So, at the time of Jesus' temptations, they were legally the devil's to offer. All he wanted in return was for Jesus to bow down and worship him.

As further proof of Satan's authority over the kingdoms of Earth, let's look into the book of Ezekiel.

> *[1] The word of the Lord came again unto me, saying,*
>
> *[2] Son of man, say unto the **prince of Tyrus**, Thus saith the Lord God; Because thine heart is lifted up, and thou hast said, I am a God, I sit in the seat of God, in the midst of the seas; **yet thou art a man**, and not God, though thou set thine heart as the heart of God:*

---

[37] 1 Timothy 2:14, Romans 5:12-21

> *[11] Moreover the word of the LORD came unto me, saying,*
>
> *[12] Son of man, take up a lamentation upon the **king of Tyrus**, and say unto him, Thus saith the Lord GOD; Thou sealest up the sum, full of wisdom, and perfect in beauty.*
>
> *[13] **Thou hast been in Eden** the garden of God; every precious stone was thy covering, the sardius, topaz, and the diamond, the beryl, the onyx, and the jasper, the sapphire, the emerald, and the carbuncle, and gold: the workmanship of thy tabrets and of thy pipes was prepared in thee in the day that thou wast created. (Ezekiel 28:1-2, and 11-13, KJV,* emphasis added*)*

When the devil tried to overthrow God's throne, he said some things kind of like this man, the Prince of Tyrus, was saying[38] in verse two. Yet, Ezekiel, writing by the inspiration of the Holy Ghost, wrote and said to this person, *"...yet thou art a man..."* So according to verse two, this man, a visible earthly king, is the Prince of Tyrus.

Did you notice that the King of Tyrus had been in Eden – the Garden of Eden? We know from the Genesis account in the Bible, that only Adam, Eve, Satan, and God were present in the Garden. Adam and Eve's children came along after they were expelled from Eden. Since the individual mentioned here in verses 12-13, the King of Tyrus, was in the Garden of Eden – he was one of the four. We know he wasn't Adam, Eve, or God. So that leaves us with Satan being the King of Tyrus.

---

[38] Isaiah 14:12-14

But, we must remember that verse two says the Prince of Tyrus is a man. This means we've got an earthly kingdom that's visible to the eye and run by a man called the Prince of Tyrus. It *also* means this visible kingdom is influenced by the invisible kingdom that is run by the devil, here called the King of Tyrus. Therefore, the devil is influencing this man, the one called the Prince of Tyrus, so that Satan can demonstrate, or prove, his authority over the earthly kingdoms.

Let's dig deeper into this:

> 3 *But if our gospel be hid, it is hid to them that are lost:*
>
> 4 ***In whom the god of this world** hath blinded the minds of them which believe not, lest the light of the glorious gospel of Christ, who is the image of God, should shine unto them. (2 Corinthians 4:3-4, KJV, emphasis added)*

When we pay close attention to detail as we read the Scriptures, we'll notice very small, but very important things. For example, in verse four, the 'g' in "god" is lowercase. This is not an accidental typo or a translation error. The original writer did this on purpose because he was not talking about God, our Father in Heaven. So then, who is the god of this world's system? Satan. We know this because of Luke 4:5-8 when he offered all the kingdoms of this world to Jesus. So, here in 2 Corinthians 4:4, we have Apostle Paul, by inspiration of the Holy Spirit, confirming that Satan is the god of this world's system.

This is important for us to understand. We live in the world, but we shouldn't operate in the world like everybody else does. Why not? Because we're from another kingdom[39]. Remember

---

[39] Colossians 1:13, John 17:15-16, John 15:19

Romans 12:2 was written to Christians to remind us not to be shaped, fashioned, and confined to think under the influence of the world. If a Christian doesn't renew his mind with the WORD and save his soul, then his mind will still be conformed to operate under the influence of the god of this world. Even though he's saved and on his way to Heaven, he will be vulnerable to the devil's influence just like the human Prince of Tyrus was influenced by the demon King of Tyrus.

Let's take a quick look at another letter Paul wrote to the Church at Ephesus on this same subject.

> *2 in which you once walked according to the course of this world, **according to the prince of the power of the air, the spirit who now works in the sons of disobedience**, (Ephesians 2:2, NKJV, emphasis added)*

Ephesians 2:2 says that we used to be subject unto the prince of the power of the air, the spirit that now worketh in the sons of disobedience in this world. I've said it before, sometimes the language of the King James and even the New King James isn't always so impactful because it is so different from the way we speak today. So let's take a look at this in the New Living Translation.

> *2 **You used to live in sin**, just like the rest of the world, **obeying the devil—the commander of the powers in the unseen world**. He is the spirit at work in the hearts of those who refuse to obey God. (Ephesians 2:2, NLT, emphasis added)*

POW! You USED to live in sin obeying the devil who is the commander of the powers of the unseen world and is the spirit at work in the hearts of those refusing to obey God. But once you are spiritually saved AND renew your mind with the WORD of

God that is not how you live any longer. We're in this world, but we shouldn't think like it and we shouldn't operate like it.

The Thief Comes to Steal, Kill, and Destroy

Now, here's the issue all Christians bump up against sooner or later – and it's usually sooner rather than later in my experience. Satan hates God and he hates God's people. He doesn't want us to have anything from God, especially anything to do with the life and character of God in abundance such as joy, peace, prosperity, divine health, or the like. So, he comes after those things to steal them, to kill them, or to destroy them in our life.

> *10 The thief cometh not, but for to steal, and to kill, and to destroy: I am come that they might have life, and that they might have it more abundantly. (John 10:10, KJV)*

Anything that comes after you to steal, to kill, or to destroy is from Satan. John 10:10 identifies who it's coming from. I recommend that you memorize this Scripture so you don't forget it. Because, sometimes, people get confused and think God is after them with a big stick. Here's an example that is all too familiar:

A guy came up to me one time and said, "Oh Brother Ricky, God almost got me!"

Now, I'm not that smart, so the Holy Ghost helped with my response and told me, "Ask him if he believes I'm perfect."

So, I obeyed, "Do you believe God is perfect?"

He answered, "I sure do."

I questioned him again, "Are you sure?"

"Absolutely!" he replied.

"Then, if He's shooting at you, Brother," I said, "He wouldn't have missed."

Always remember this key concept: anything that's stealing, killing, or destroying is coming from the thief. Because Jesus said, "...I *am come that they might have life...*" Furthermore, the life that Jesus came to bring us is the very nature, character, and eternal life of God. Jesus said, He came, "*...so that they might have life and that they might have it more abundantly.*"

The Soul is the Battlefield

As Christians, we believe according to Romans 8:17 that we are heirs of God and joint-heirs with Christ. Now, let's look at the letter written to the church at Galatia (but also to us[40]):

> [1] Now I say, That the **heir**, as long as he is a **child**, differeth nothing from a servant, though he be lord of all;
>
> [2] But is under tutors and governors until the time appointed of the father.
>
> [3] Even so we, when we were children, were **in bondage under the elements of the world**: (Galatians 4:1-3, KJV, emphasis added)

In verse three, the word "elements" means "circumstances." It's talking about every wind that comes along dictating to you how you are going to act. This is painting a picture of someone being led by their emotions. Sometimes, a person will say, "My emotions are just running away with themselves," or, "I

---

[40] I believe Apostle Paul wrote the book of Galatians. He spoke it and someone recorded it for him, but it was through him that God wrote this letter to the Galatians.

just don't know what's going on with my emotions today." One minute they are laughing, the next crying, and then right after that, they're mad as a wet hen. They'll be hot and then cold and everything else, all in between.

Remember, saving the soul is a process. It is important to understand that our soul has not been saved it is *being* saved.

> *39 But we are not of them who draw back unto **perdition**; but of them that **believe to the saving of the soul.** (Hebrews 10:39, KJV, emphasis added)*

Let's look at it in the Weymouth ("WNT") translation as well:

> *39 But we are not people who shrink back and perish, but are among those who **believe and gain possession of their souls**. (Hebrews 10:39, WNT, emphasis added)*

Drawing back unto perdition means going back to old habits and lifestyles one had before salvation. If we want to live victorious lives, we cannot go backwards. We must keep renewing our minds with the WORD so we can continually move onward and upward through the individual plan of God for our lives. God put emotions in us for a reason, but He doesn't want us to be ruled by them. He wants us to walk in divine health. He wants everything we touch to increase. God wants you to be victorious.

> *29 For he that eateth and drinketh unworthily, eateth and drinketh damnation to himself, not discerning the Lord's body.*
>
> *30 **For this cause many are weak and sickly among you, and many sleep.** (1 Corinthians 11:29-30, KJV, emphasis added)*

In dealing with difficult situations, the hardest places you will ever have to deal with the devil are in your soul and in your body. But usually, before it is ever in your body it is in your soul (your mind, your will, and your emotions) because that is where the battlefield is located. If you can get that thing (anger, offense, unforgiveness, or whatever it is) dealt with while it is in your soul, then you can learn to laugh, and dance, and shout when all hell is breaking out around you.

Right now it looks like the whole world is going to hell in a hand basket. It seems like it's shaking, rattling, and rolling everywhere. Don't worry about it. It's going to last as long as we need it to. We're at the right place doing the right thing always. I'll say it again, church life, Christian life in general, ought to be the happiest, funniest, greatest, most joyful experience ever. I know there are times when we have to be serious, but when our mind is properly renewed, we can enjoy hanging out with folks who enjoy their salvation. That's victory!

Chapter 5 – You Can be Free

It's not always going to be a cakewalk in this life. There are going to be ups and downs – hills and valleys. To be victorious in this life, it's really important to keep everything on the happy side. We might as well laugh all the way through. Let's just have a ball. I've tried being all serious, but I find it just doesn't work as well as being happy. Being happy is a lot better – especially when you're laughing your way through troubles.

Talk to the Pressure

Now there are times when the pressure of a situation gets heavy on you. But there are ways to get out from underneath it. First, don't just *think about it*. You cannot destroy a thought with another thought. You must *talk to it with words*. So, when a thought comes that is contrary to the Bible, if you have been studying the Bible and have renewed your mind, then you can answer that thought thoroughly by speaking the Scripture. Dr. Lester Sumrall is a perfect example of this:

In Demons, The Answer Book, Dr. Lester Sumrall wrote about a time when he was ministering in the Philippines. Eventually, a church was established there, but at this time there was a crazy lady there causing trouble. The police had arrested her and she was in jail. Yet something would attack her. They couldn't see what was attacking her, but they could see the teeth and scratch marks on her.

Finally, God directed Dr. Sumrall to go down and take care of that situation with her. He obeyed God and went. The first time he walked in this little Filipino lady cussed him out and said stuff about his momma in English. But, once she was delivered and saved, she could never talk English again. It was by that devil that she was speaking English. That spirit said some very accusing things to Dr. Sumrall about his momma and he didn't let it go. He said, "You are a liar. My mother is not a whore. My mother was married to my father." He went down line by line and discredited what that devil said (Sumrall).

From this example, we learn when the devil says something to you like, "You're not going to make it this time." Don't just say, "I resist you," or, "Shut up in Jesus' name." No. You must defeat that thought completely so that it will not come back to you. Therefore, you go line by line and answer that entire thing that he said and defeat it with the WORD. You tell him, "I can do all things through Christ[41]. I am the head and not the tail. I am above and not beneath[42]. I will get to the other side[43]." I mean you answer it entirely with the WORD. Now, the devil might *try* to bring it back again. But once you have answered it entirely and defeated it with Scripture, as far as you're concerned, it is a total lie and it's dealt with.

The battlefield is in the mind. Brother Kenneth E. Hagin used to always teach us that if you can keep the devil in the arena of faith, you will whip him every single time. But if he can get you in the arena of the soul, he will whip you.

---

[41] Philippians 4:13

[42] Deuteronomy 28:13

[43] Mark 4:35

But, you have to know, it takes a renewed mind to do that. Because when you first come off of a habit such as drinking, drugs, smoking, worry, or anything like that, the greatest battlefield isn't necessarily with the flesh. It's with the thoughts. It's dealing with the enemy's suggestions that you ought to go back to that thing you just came off.

The WORD Will Make You Free

The devil loves to trick believers. We have to be very alert and vigilant about what we let in through our ear gates and eye gates. We also have to make sure that we pay close attention to the WORD. Let's look at Adam and Eve as an example:

> [15] *And the LORD God took the man, and* **put him into the garden of Eden to dress it and to keep it.**
>
> [16] *And The LORD God commanded the man, saying, Of every tree of the garden thou mayest freely eat:*
>
> [17] *But of the* **tree of the knowledge of good and evil,** *thou shalt not eat of it:* **for in the day that thou eatest thereof thou shalt surely die.** *(Genesis 2:15-17, KJV, emphasis added)*

Keeping in mind everything God said to Adam, now look at Genesis 3.

> [3]*Now the serpent was more subtle than any beast of the field which The LORD God had made. And he said unto the woman, Yea, hath God said,* **Ye shall not eat of every tree of the garden?** *(Genesis 3:1, KJV, emphasis added)*

When we read this very closely, we see that the serpent is already distorting what God said. He said to the woman, *"Yea, hath God said, Ye shall not eat of every tree of the garden?"* Did God say that? No. He said you can eat of every tree but one specific tree. Look at what the serpent said again, *"Ye shall not eat of **every tree?**"* You need to know what the Bible says. Because Satan is good at twisting it just a little bit. But when it is twisted just a little bit, many times that is enough to trick people into wrong thinking. The "appointed time to die" doctrine[44] is a great example of this.

Now, let's look at the woman's response to the serpent.

> *2 And the woman said unto the serpent, We may eat of the fruit of the trees of the garden:*
>
> *3 But of the fruit of the tree which is in the midst of the garden, God hath said, Ye shall not eat of it, **neither shall ye touch it**, lest ye die. (Genesis 3:2-3, KJV, emphasis added)*

Truly, I don't know if God said that or not. But the Scripture doesn't say He did. So, I don't know if she added it or if she's just thinking about touching it. Either way it's important to say Scripture accurately. For example, you may have heard, "Cleanliness is next to godliness." But is it scriptural? No. It is not in the Bible. It's a good saying and it has truth to it. But it is not scriptural.

> *32 And **ye shall know the truth**, and the truth shall make you free. (John 8:32, KJV, emphasis added)*

There is also a difference between natural fact and truth.

---

44 Hebrews 9:27 *(Discussed in greater detail in Chapter 2.)*

*¹⁷ Sanctify them through thy truth: **thy word is truth**. (John 17:17, KJV, emphasis added)*

According to John 8:32, why will the truth set us free? Because we know Jesus? No! It says we'll be free because we **know the truth**. Furthermore, from John 17:17, we know that God's Word is truth. Now I have a question for you. In mathematics, does 2+2=4? Yes. That's a true fact in the natural sense. But is it a truth in the scriptural sense? No, it's not.

You know, I tried that on the devil and it did not faze him. I discovered that just because you know a natural fact, it will never help you defeat the devil. He can come after you in some area of your life and you can shout to him, "2+2=4!" with all the authority and courage you can muster. And he'll be like, "Okay....and?"

So, it can't be a good saying, a natural fact, or even a natural truth that will make you free. It must be *the* truth or the WORD of God. Sometimes, I'm amazed at how little Scripture the Body of Christ actually knows that is solid New Testament WORD of God. You have to **know** *the WORD* – not doctrine, not theory, not experience, and not opinion. Folks, the devil will beat your brains out if all you scream at him is, "Water freezes at 32°!" or "2+2=4!" But when we are like Jesus in Matthew chapter four and we say, "Devil, it is written...," then he'll get his hands off us pretty quickly. Undoubtedly, the devil is depending on ignorance for him to work his plan in a Christian's life. We must be careful not to educate our heads at the expense of our hearts.

It has to be by the WORD. We must know the truth of the WORD. Some people know a lot of facts about medical science. But facts won't heal you. Quite the opposite in fact, that medical knowledge really fights against people when it comes to receiving divine healing. Same thing goes for prosperity. Some people think they need to move someplace prosperous in order to prosper. But, we have to remember if God told you to be in a certain place, then that place is your Garden of Eden – not someplace else.

When we put these three verses together, we come to understand that Jesus was telling us, "You shall know the WORD, and it will make you free because you know it."

Now, let's dig a little deeper:

> 28 *Come unto me, all ye that labour and are heavy laden, and I will give you rest.*
>
> 29 *Take my yoke upon you, and learn of me; for I am meek and lowly in heart: and* **ye shall find rest unto your souls**. *(Matthew 11:28-29, KJV, emphasis added)*

Rest, in the soul (mind, will, and emotions), comes from learning of Jesus – not simply from being saved. When we were saved, we were made free. But that freedom does not encompass all three parts of the human being – spirit, soul, and body. It was freedom for one part – our spirit. Paul's message throughout all of the epistles was simple, "The provision for a Christian to live completely free has been completely purchased and paid for by Jesus." This is why Jesus said, in John 8:32, *"You shall know the truth and the truth shall make you free" (NKJV)*. Knowing the true WORD of God sets us free in the soul.

> 36 *If the Son therefore shall make you free, ye shall be free indeed. (John 8:36, KJV)*

The freedom we need – everything we need to live completely free – Jesus has already purchased. But just because He purchased it doesn't mean we have it automatically just because we got saved. He finished the work that was required for all humanity to be free. Yet all of humanity is not free. Freedom

60

comes through knowledge. And knowledge can only be gained with an investment of time and dedication to learn what Jesus did and what He made available by His sacrifice.

You Have to Want to be Free

We have a lot of people that come to our church that are ordered to go for drug and alcohol treatment. In our town it's very unique. The judge will order them to various treatments such as AA[45], counseling, DUI School, and etc. One time, the judge told a guy, "If you'll go out to that church," meaning Family Worship Center, "I'll count it as part of your class on Wednesday nights." So we'll have people come and they'll sit. Sometimes, they're drunker than Cooter Brown[46]. I don't know too much about Cooter Brown, but they're drunker and sitting right there on the second row while either my wife or I are preaching. It doesn't bother me too much, because I used to be where they are and I know you can get out of it.

One night I was preaching a real good message and a guy said, "I don't believe that!"

Most of these people are like him. They tell me, "I can't get out of that – it's got a hold of me too hard." Well then, let's just rip the Bible up right now! I'm telling you there is a way out! Most of these people that we deal with love God, they love Him with all

---

[45] Alcoholics Anonymous

[46] The legend of Cooter Brown is that he lived on the dividing line between the North and South during the Civil War making him eligible for draft by both sides. He didn't want to fight for one reason or another. So, he decided he would stay so continuously drunk he would be useless to either side for the duration of the war (Cooter Brown).

their heart, but they never took time to get their soul saved. Therefore, their soul always sides with their body. The inside of them, their spirit man, is born again and screaming, "No, No, No!"

Look, I wasn't considered an alcoholic by the law because I didn't have to attend AA. I was just a drunk. The last time I got a DUI, I was in Stillwater, OK. That's where Oklahoma State University is located. When I came to, a cop was dragging me out of the truck. I asked him, "Well, what have I done?"

He's shaking his head like, "Well, you've been sitting here through three red lights."

I was good friends with most, if not all, of the cops back then. In fact, you could say I was on a first name basis with them. They loved being a limousine service for me. I'd ride around in the back and they'd drive me all around.

People used to tell me, "You know, you'll never get out of it."

But I tell you what, the WORD of God is TRUTH. I've seen people with cancer, with leukemia, with blood disease, and all kinds of things – I've seen every one of them walk away from it and be fully made whole. God can do miraculous things. But here's the thing. If you get saved because you are facing death or prison, but you never take time to get your soul saved, the devil will so fight your mind, your will, and your emotions, that you'll never get victory. With an unrenewed mind, you'll have no defense for devilish lies such as, "Well, you know you'll never really stop drinking or you'll never stop doing drugs..." or "You're not going to get well." Life is better if you'll just believe the WORD and do what it says, then you'll know you can have anything that's in it.

I tell you, we've been in meetings where a lot of people have joint trouble – and I'm not talking about arthritic joints either. They'll be sitting in service with dark glasses on smiling all big and I'm like, "Yeah, whatever, you're not even here. You're higher than a Georgia Pine." I know because I've been there. I know what it's like. But I'm telling you this WORD that's called the Bible – it is the TRUTH. And if you want to be free, you can be free, but you've got to have the want to. These men and women that come to our place on Wednesday night, many keep coming back once they are released out of treatment. They tell us, "We got free, but now we want to live free." God is a good God.

A lot of people hear me talk about drugs and alcohol and they can't relate. They tell me, "Well, Pastor Ricky, that's all good, but I'm not a drinker and I don't do drugs." But you know what? Sometimes we live in bondage to poverty, or fear, or worry over a kid or a grandkid. Whether it's worry that your husband's going to die and leave you alone, or whatever else, that's fear and torment. There's no need living there either.

> [7] casting all your care upon Him, for He
> cares for you. (1 Peter 5:7, NKJV)

When I start talking about worry, people come to me and say things like, "Well, you know Brother Ricky, nobody cares." Ok. But God does, and other people do too. I'm telling you worry doesn't work and it'll kill the human body. You ought to live life laughing. We should not be worrying about stuff.

Grace Only Works on Us if We Work with It

The grace of God made salvation and abundant victory available. But how do we access what grace is providing? The answer is Ephesians 2:4-8 – we access it through faith.

⁴ But God, who is rich in mercy, for his great love wherewith he loved us,

*⁵ **Even when we were dead in sins, hath quickened us together with Christ, (by grace ye are saved;)***

⁶ And hath raised us up together, and made us sit together in heavenly places in Christ Jesus:

*⁷ That in the ages to come he might shew the exceeding riches of his **grace** in his kindness **toward us through Christ Jesus.***

*⁸ **For by grace are ye saved through faith**; and that not of yourselves: it is the gift of God: (Ephesians 2:4-8, KJV, emphasis added)*

Let's jump over to Romans 5 and see what Paul had to say about this subject. We'll come back to Ephesians 2 in a moment.

*¹Therefore being **justified by faith**, we have peace with God through our Lord Jesus Christ: (Romans 5:1, KJV, emphasis added)*

"Justified by faith" means it's just as if we have never done anything wrong. Say out loud, "I'm sure glad I'm the righteousness of God. God sees me just as if I'd never sinned. Amen." We can say that because we're spiritually saved[47].

So, with the definition of justified inserted, Romans 5:1 could read like this, "Therefore, being just as if we've never done anything wrong by faith and through that faith we have peace with

---

[47] If you've never asked Jesus into your heart, then turn to Appendix 1 in the back of the book and take care of that right now. There's no time like the present.

God through our LORD Jesus Christ." Aren't you glad God ain't mad at us! I know I am!

> *2 By whom also **we have access by faith into this grace** wherein we stand, and rejoice in hope of the glory of God. (Romans 5:2, KJV, emphasis added)*

Now let's look at what Paul told the church at Corinth but also to you and I today:

> *But by the **grace of God I am what I am**: and his grace which was bestowed ,upon me was not in vain; but **I laboured** more abundantly than they all: yet not I, but the grace of God which was with me. (1 Corinthians 15:10, KJV, emphasis added)*

I have always loved this particular scripture. Notice Paul did not say that the grace of God made Paul what he was apart from Paul. In other words, it wasn't God on Paul making him into something that he did not agree to be. Nor was it all God with Paul just sitting there saying, "God you're going to do all of this for me." Paul had to use his faith to cooperate with the grace of God to fulfill the plan of God for his life.

Remember, we just read in Ephesians and Romans that it always required faith to get into what grace provided. So if grace is going to make you or I something without any cooperation from us, then it would override our free will. And, I can't find anywhere in Scriptures where God ever does that. Yet, I know, through other examples God will provide things by grace that not everyone will access. For example, salvation is available by the grace of God, yet not everyone is saved. Why not? Because everyone has free will and gets to make the choice to accept what God is offering or not. So it requires faith on our part to get into what grace is providing.

So, when Paul said, "I am what I am by the grace of God..." he must have come into agreement with what God's grace on him had called him to be. Furthermore, by him getting into grace, he labored to get there. It wasn't the power of God instantly transforming Paul. No. God told Paul what he was and what He wanted him to be. But, it took Paul working with God and the grace of God to get Paul to the final destination.

Practically speaking, that means if you want to walk out of some kind of bondage, you're going to have to renew your mind with the WORD of God and you're going to have to listen to the Holy Spirit. He will put godly men and women in your path to help you. He will speak to you through His WORD and through them. Through His WORD and through these mentors, He'll tell you specific things to do such as: don't go back to that place, don't go around those people anymore, go across town to buy your gas, make amends to that person, go to that church, and etc. Do it all. Brother Hagin used to say, "Faith is like a door that swings on two hinges: listen and obey." As you listen and obey you are using your faith to work with the grace of God to come out of that place of bondage and into the place of freedom.

Chapter 6 – Yokes Aren't for Humans

The Anchor for Our Soul

The WORD should put an end to all strife, both internal and external, based on the promises for New Testament Christians[48]. The Bible is our answer. So, if I'm arguing with the Bible, then I'm arguing with my answer. Let's take a look at two things Jesus said about how to handle the storms and pressures of this life.

> *"Don't let your hearts be troubled. Trust in God, and trust also in me. (John 14:1, NLT)*
>
> [29] ***Take my yoke upon you,*** *and **learn of me**; for I am meek and lowly in heart: and ye shall find **rest unto your souls**. (Matthew 11:29, KJV, emphasis added)*

Remember, most of the time, the word "heart" in the Bible is referring to the soul. So, in John 14:1, Jesus is saying when the storms and pressures of life come against us, they will try to trouble our souls (mind, will, and emotions). He not only reminded us to trust in God and Him, but He also told us to learn His ways and to take up His yoke so we could find rest for our souls.

But it is deeper than that. In order to do what Jesus asks, we have to *know* that God will keep His WORD and fulfill the promises that we learn about as we renew our minds:

---

[48] Hebrews 6:16-20

*16 Now when people take an oath, they call on someone greater than themselves to hold them to it. And without any question that oath is binding. 17 God also bound himself with an oath, so that **those who received the promise could be perfectly sure that he would never change his mind.** 18 So God has given both his promise and his oath. These two things are unchangeable because **it is impossible for God to lie.** Therefore, we who have fled to him for refuge can have great confidence as we hold to the hope that lies before us. 19 **This hope is a strong and trustworthy anchor for our souls.** It leads us through the curtain into God's inner sanctuary. 20 Jesus has already gone in there for us. He has become our eternal High Priest in the order of Melchizedek. (Hebrews 6:16-20, NLT, emphasis added)*

God understands that we have to know we can trust Him. That's why He gave an oath so that we could be perfectly sure He would never change His mind about anything He ever promised us in His WORD. It is impossible for God to lie. Pay close attention here, it is by learning of Him, not ONLY by being saved, but by *learning* of Him, who He is, what He has done, and what He has promised that gives you an anchor in your emotions when the storms come. Renewing your mind with the WORD keeps your soul steady.

37 For yet a little while, and he that shall come will come, and will not tarry.

38 Now the just shall live by faith: but if any man draw back, my soul shall have no pleasure in him.

39 But we are not of them who draw back unto perdition; but of them that believe to the saving of the soul. (Hebrews 10:37-39 KJV)

Brother Hagin used to say, "When a Christian gets their soul saved and renewed with the WORD of God, it will help them because it will agree with the faith that is in their heart." Just like a car works by gas, your faith works by love[49]. These things all join together: faith, love, and renewing the mind to keep you moving forward.

But look at verses 38 and 39 again. What made those Christians draw back? Their souls. Remember, that's where the battle is and where the onslaught will be the worst. If you don't continually renew your mind, you won't be battle ready. Brother Hagin used to warn us, "If you keep the devil in the arena of faith, you'll whip him every time. But, if you allow him to pull you into the arena of reasoning, he'll whip you every time."

Yokes of All Kinds

Have you ever seen two oxen yoked together in those old movies? I grew up a country boy. I live in the city now and you can tell. But, since I grew up in the country, I know what real physical yokes are. I've seen them before. My dad had some. Some yokes hook two animals to each other and some tie an unruly animal to one spot so he can't wander off and hurt someone or himself. No matter if they are single or double, they come in two kinds: wooden and iron. Yokes have a great big U-bolt, so you can lay them over the neck of the animal and tighten them up with a pin on it. Whatever the animal is tied to, that's where he's going to go. So, if he's yoked to another animal, the two have no choice but to go in the same direction.

---

49 Galatians 5:6

Many times people get saved, filled with the Holy Ghost, and get hooked up with a church that teaches the whole Bible. But their thinking stays all goofed up even though they are being taught everything they need to know. Why is that? As we've already seen, saved people can still be influenced by the god of this world and can be focusing on things they ought not to be thinking about. This is why Jesus encourages us to be yoked to Him and learn from Him:

> *29 Take my yoke upon you, and learn of me; for I am meek and lowly in heart: and ye shall find rest unto your souls. (Matthew 11:29, KJV)*

If Jesus is telling us to take His yoke upon us, it means that we can be yoked to other things. Paul further cautions us not to be unequally yoked together in 2 Corinthians 6:14. Let's look at this verse:

> *+ Be ye not unequally yoked together with unbelievers: for what fellowship hath righteousness with unrighteousness? and what communion hath light with darkness? (2 Corinthians 6:14, KJV)*

Most everyone that reads this verse understands it means believers should not marry unbelievers. But, there's more to it. He's telling us believers can be yoked to other things and ideas and we better be alert.

Sometimes, people get saved and think, "Whoo-hoo! I'm on my way to Heaven! Jesus set me free!"

When we ask, "Well, what do you know about Scripture?"

"Not a bloomin' thing, but I'm on my way to Heaven!" they'll cheerfully reply.

I'm here to warn you, if you do nothing else and you live that way the rest of your life, you will probably get to Heaven sooner than the rest of us. When the devil had you, he wasn't very concerned about you. However, your salvation changed that because it made you his direct enemy. Now, he wants you to stay yoked up with incorrect thinking. If he can get you to do that, then he can keep you bound and down, rather than victoriously living days of Heaven on Earth.

Don't Be Unequally Yoked

As I previously mentioned, we've had several people come to our ministry that are struggling with alcohol, drugs, or something like that. They might or might not be in treatment. As I've watched these folks, I've noticed a pattern. Everything will go along alright for about nine weeks or so and then they'll kind of hit a plateau. At that point, if there is no progression with the soul, we've seen they usually don't make it. They go back as the dog goes back to its vomit[50]. It's not a question of them being saved. They're saved and they love Jesus. But with an unrenewed mind they won't live victoriously. So, why is it so difficult for them to break free when they're saved and they love Jesus?

Remember, the truth Jesus was speaking of in John 8:32 is the truth of God's WORD. Additionally, remember that in Matthew 11:28-29, Jesus said, *"Come unto me all ye that labor and are heavy laden and I'll give you rest. Take **my yoke** upon you and learn of me" (KJV).* We know that in order to be born again spiritually, one must come in contact with the Blood of Jesus, because it took the Blood of Jesus to make us able to be made spiritually alive unto God. But just being saved does not make us

---

50 Proverbs 26:11

victorious. That's why Jesus said in John 8, "Know the truth and by knowing the truth it will make you free" *(vs. 32)*. Now, in 2 Corinthians 6, we are warned not to be *unequally yoked together* because light cannot have agreement with darkness[51]. When we take these three verses together, we start to understand that people's souls can get yoked with wrong thinking.

When the soul is yoked to wrong thinking, it causes internal strife in the person. Their physical body has a craving for something and their mind says, "Yeah, that's exactly what I need!" But the whole time, their spirit man is screaming, "Oh no! I quit that! I'm saved! I don't want that anymore!" But the soul and the flesh gang up on the spirit and hold it hostage because 2/3 majority wins.

The only way to get off the roller coaster and to get rid of the internal strife is to change their thinking about that thing with the WORD of God. Then it will agree with the faith in their heart and they'll have victory, peace, and rest. Hebrews 6:18-19 tell us there is an anchor for the soul and it is the promises of God and the oath of God. When they grab hold of those promises of God, the strife and discord inside them will begin to disappear.

Drugs and alcohol aren't the only carnal, or flesh, issues people need to be set free from. This unequal yoking and internal strife presents itself in all sorts of ways. People have come up to me and said, "Well, I don't believe we can be rich."

"OK. Be poor." I'm serious about it! Because the Bible says in 2 Corinthians that Jesus became poor so that we might be made rich[52].

---

[51] 2 Corinthians 6:14

[52] 2 Corinthians 8:9

72

To which they usually retort, "Well, Brother Ricky, that just means spiritually."

I can agree with that. But, if I'm rich spiritually, it ought to show up in my physical body and I ought to walk in health. Everything I touch ought to prosper and grow. So then, it will affect every other area of my life, but if you believe you have to be poor to be righteous, then you are yoked with wrong thinking.

Sometimes people will say, "Well you know, I know God *can* heal, but I'm not sure He *wants* to heal me." Well, read Isaiah 53, Matthew 8, and 1 Peter 2:24 to settle that matter. I truly believe healing comes every time. If somebody dies sick, it wasn't because it was God's will. The WORD should put an end to that kind of internal strife.

For example, I remember back to the time when we held some meetings down in southeast Texas. The Holy Spirit had me teaching on healing rather than preaching. A lady was brought to the meetings straight from the hospital. She sat in these teachings and soaked it all in. Nobody ever laid hands on her. Then, after just sitting there, she took the oxygen off and her lungs were completely made whole and new. Before coming to the meetings, she had believed that God made people sick to teach them some kind of lesson through sickness. After the teachings, she had changed her mind to agree with the WORD, removed the oxygen, and was completely healed. You see even though she was saved, born again, and on her way to Heaven, since her mind wasn't renewed to divine health, her soul joined sides with her flesh and kept her stuck in the carnal arena of sickness.

Let me share an example of how I was unequally yoked in my own thinking. I was yoked to a poverty mentality, because we were raised kind of poor. When my wife and I got saved someone helped us with different things and told us we ought to go to Rhema, and then they helped us get there. When we started, I didn't know "come here" from "sic 'em". I mean I didn't know nothing!

At Rhema, they talked a lot about prosperity belonging to the believer. I struggled with this teaching because I just kept remembering back to that doctrine about it's easier for a camel to go through the eye of a needle than it is for a rich man to get into Heaven[53]. I didn't know where it was in the Bible and I had no idea what it meant, but I knew you shouldn't have anything. See, I was yoked to something that wasn't scriptural.

Now, on this flip side of this coin, I was healthy. I stayed after healing for five years on some things and then went after it even longer than that in some other areas. I listened to some teachings 150 times or more. Every time I would listen, I'd hear something else. Finally, the LORD asked me one day, "What are you going to do about prosperity?"

I answered, "Well, to be honest with you, I wasn't going to do anything about it."

"You're going to need to. You're a healthy little booger, but you're so broke you can't get out of town," He replied. (Keep in mind, God talks to each of us in the lingo we best understand and I understood Him right away.)

So I said, "Okay LORD, I'll get after it," and I immediately started studying prosperity to make His thoughts on it my thoughts on it.

---

[53] Matthew 19:24

Oh my goodness! I'd run into stuff in the WORD of God and I'd see where God wanted me rich and there was so much in me that was contrary to that. All that contrariness was a yoke of bondage. But the anointing of God destroys yokes. A lot of times people just think of yokes in terms of devils or sickness. But they can be wrong thinking as well.

In the end, you know what I found out about prosperity? You can't quantify "rich" as a million dollars, two million, three million, etc. Rich is a full supply that transcends money. It's not up to God whether you live healthy or wealthy, because Jesus already purchased everything you need to be fully supplied in *every* area of your life. It all hinges on the way you think.

By being saved, you are qualified for the *entire* inheritance. But if you never get your mind renewed with the WORD of God to save your soul, then your spirit and soul will never agree and you'll have a fight on your hands. Your spirit man, where the Spirit of God resides, is shouting, "Yes, that's right! Take it by faith!" But your unrenewed soul is retorting, "No, I don't think so..." When you have this internal strife, dig into the Word on the subject and start to renew your mind. As you do, your soul will start to agree with your spirit.

It's important to understand this is why we must take care of our soul daily just like we take care of our body. Your mind will always lapse back to its old ways of thinking. It won't stay renewed any more than your hair will stay combed. You must keep your hair combed every day, so what must you do with your mind every day? Renew it with the WORD of God. Comb your hair every day and renew your soul every day. Brother Hagin used to say, "If you show me a spiritual giant, I'll show you somebody whose soul and spirit agree."

Stay Out of the Locoweed

While we are the subject of yokes, let's take a look at shepherds. If you've been around the church or Christians any length of time, you're probably familiar with the 23rd Psalm. It's the one that starts out, *"The LORD is my shepherd..."* Jesus is at the right hand of the Father, so how can He be my shepherd if He doesn't live here anymore? I'm glad you asked. King David[54] and Apostle Paul[55] both addressed this. But for now, let's look at the Letter to the Ephesians.

> [8] *Wherefore he saith, When he ascended up on high, he led captivity captive, and gave gifts unto men. (Ephesians 4:8, KJV)*

When Jesus was here, He walked in all five ministry offices: apostle, prophet, pastor, teacher, and evangelist. But He said, "I'm getting ready to go. And when I go, I'm going to lead captivity captive and give these gifts unto men." The gifts He's talking about are the ministry offices operating through human vessels.

Many people say, "Well, the LORD is my shepherd." I understand. But everyone needs to have a pastor here as well. Let me further explain some of the things Jesus was referring to that a shepherd will do for his flock. For one, they lead the flock to green pastures. In other words, they make sure the flock is fed and

---

54 Psalm 68:18

55 Ephesians 4:8

76

watered properly. I'll use an example from my own life to illustrate.

Years ago, my dad had a place in Blackburn, OK. He bought some big old Hereford cows off my Uncle Bob. Herefords are big and gentle rascals. They were so gentle you could even pet them. One time my dad turned them loose on the property for a few days. But when we went back to gather them up, the minute they saw us coming, they raised their tails up over their backs like white-tail deer and took off into the brush. Those gentle cows had gotten into some locoweed, which is similar to marijuana, and they went crazy. We eventually had to go get cowboys with horses to chase them down – we even had to tranquilize a few with a dart gun. See, they ate the wrong food. It was inappropriate for them.

When the WORD of God is coming through the Office of the Shepherd, it will be food that is nutritious to the flock. You won't be led astray. But, when you don't have a shepherd on Earth to teach you the WORD, you could end up eating the wrong stuff and the next thing we know, you're loco like those cows.

The second verse of the 23rd Psalm says, *"He maketh me to lie down in green pastures: he leadeth me beside the still waters" (KJV)*. This is speaking of rest for your soul. When you come to church and you listen to the pastor teach you, you're learning of Jesus. You're finding rest for your soul. See, it takes Jesus to be saved. Since our soul doesn't get saved with our spirits, we don't want to be yoked to anything in our thinking that doesn't give us rest or that causes internal strife.

Chapter 7 – Except a Man be Born of Water and of Spirit

The Fall of Man Changed our Spirit Nature

When Adam partook of the fruit, he not only sinned and died spiritually, but the nature of his spirit was changed. That change was then passed down to all humanity and required a perfect atonement to restore humanity to its previous relationship with God[56]. Let's look more carefully at how the nature of man was changed at the fall.

> *¹And you hath he **quickened**, who were dead in **trespasses and sins**;*
>
> *² Wherein in time past ye walked according to the course of this world, **according to the prince of the power of the air, the spirit that now worketh in the children of disobedience:** (Ephesians 2:1-2, KJV, emphasis added)*

The word "quickened" in Ephesians 2:1 is an Old English word that means "to make alive" or "made alive". When I used to shoe horses, if the nail turned the wrong way, you'd know it once you put his foot down because he'd sort of wiggle and jump. He wouldn't be able to put any pressure on that foot, and that meant you drove that nail in wrong and you got it into the quick. Well, what does "quick" mean? You got into the place where it's alive. That's the same Old English word.

---

[56] Romans 5:12-21

So, we were spiritually dead and separated from God. He goes on to show us, in verse two, that there is a spirit working in those that do not know God. Let's continue on:

> *3 Among whom also we all had our **conversation** in times past **in the lusts of our flesh, fulfilling the desires of the flesh and of the mind**; and were by nature the children of wrath, even as others. (Ephesians 2:3, KJV, emphasis added)*

Verse three is packed with important information. The word "conversation" doesn't mean a discussion or a chat like we use it today. When you look it up, it is more closely related to "lifestyle" (Interlinear Bible). I hope, when you read this verse you quickly recognized that the phrases *"lusts of our flesh"* and *"desires of the flesh and of the mind"* both refer to an unrenewed mind joining forces with the body. In fact, this verse is so important, you should underline it or highlight[57] in your Bible so you don't forget it.

Read Ephesians 2:3 again carefully in the Amplified Classic ("AMPC") translation:

> *3Among these we as well as you once lived and conducted ourselves in the passions of our flesh [our behavior governed by our corrupt and sensual nature], obeying the impulses of the flesh and the thoughts of the mind [our cravings dictated by our senses and our dark imaginings]. We were **then by nature children of [God's] wrath and heirs of [His] indignation, like the rest of mankind**. (Ephesians 2:3, AMP, emphasis added)*

---

[57] A simple yellow crayon works great for highlighting without bleeding through.

Notice that little word "then". Remember it. It's very important. We *used* to have a sinful nature. We received it at the fall of man. At that time, *"We were then by nature children of [God's] wrath and heirs of [His] indignation, like the rest of mankind,"* **and then** we got born again spiritually.

Some modern translations help us to see more clearly where that sinful nature really came from. Let's look at a couple:

> *All of us used to be just as they are,* ***our lives expressing the evil within us,*** *doing every wicked thing that our passions or our evil thoughts might lead us into. We started out bad, being born with evil natures, and were under God's anger just like everyone else. (Ephesians 2:3, The Living Bible "TLB",* emphasis added)

> *We were all guilty of falling headlong for the persuasive passions of this world; we all have had our fill of indulging the flesh and mind,* ***obeying impulses to follow perverse thoughts motivated by dark powers.*** *As a result, our natural inclinations led us to be children of wrath, just like the rest of humankind. (Ephesians 2:3, The Voice Bible,* emphasis added)

I point this out because, sometimes, people think that fallen nature was only in their body or in their soul. I know I did too until God asked me about it one day[58]. Up until that day, I always thought the lower nature, or the fallen nature, which we received in the Garden of Eden was either the body (which never gets saved)

---

[58] If God asks you a question, keep in mind, it isn't because He doesn't know the answer. He's trying to get you to walk in a deeper revelation. He's showing you that the revelation you have either isn't complete or it isn't correct.

or the soul (which must get renewed). That was partially correct, but I didn't have the whole the picture.

That day God asked me, "What filled Lucifer's[59] heart once he decided to overthrow my throne?" According to Ezekiel 28:15 he was full of violence.

Then God asked, "*Where* was he full of violence?" Since Lucifer did not possess a body, the violence had to be in his spirit. There's no other option. Therefore, when Adam fell in the Garden of Eden, what separated him from God was *spiritual* separation. He took on a different nature – the life and nature of Satan (or death) was imparted into his spirit. This seed of spiritual death would eventually infect the soul and the body and lead to physical death as well[60].

Your Reborn Spirit – the Holy Ghost's Home

Sin and death came into the world by one man's sin – Adam's. Grace, forgiveness, and life came into the world through one man's death – Christ's[61]. Christ came to fix the damage done to our spirits and to restore our unfettered access to God the Father. Remember, according to Ephesians 2:1, before Jesus, mankind was dead in our trespasses and sins because we had a fallen nature.

God could have chosen any form for the crowning jewel of his creation, but He chose to make us spirit beings just like

[59] Lucifer became known as Satan after the fall from heaven. (Ezekiel 28:6-17, Isaiah 14:12-14, & Revelation 20:1-10)

[60] For more information about Satan and his interaction with Heaven today see Appendix 2

[61] Romans 5:12-21

Himself. In 1 Corinthians 6:19, we learn that God did this for a special purpose – so that we would be the home of his Spirit.

> *19 What? know ye not that your body is the temple of the Holy Ghost which is in you, which ye have of God, and ye are not your own? (1 Corinthians 6:19, KJV)*

Today, we know when someone asks Jesus Christ into his life, the Holy Ghost, also known as the Holy Spirit, enters that person at that moment. It may have been a prayer as simple as, "Jesus, I believe you're the Son of God. I believe you died. I believe you rose again. I ask you to come into my life." It doesn't matter *how* the person asks. The important part is his confession of faith in Jesus and what Jesus did for him.

Follow me carefully here. When a person makes a confession of faith in Jesus and what He did, the Holy Ghost does not come to make just the person's *body* his temple. No, the Holy Ghost comes to dwell and to commune with the real man – the spirit man – who lives *inside* the body. Therefore, *our spirit inside the body* is the temple of the Holy Ghost and His home.

This means the Holy Ghost lives inside of us and He joins with and communicates with our spirit. He doesn't join with and communicate with our body because the Holy Ghost isn't a body. He doesn't join with and communicate with our mind because the Holy Ghost isn't a mind either. He is a spirit, so He always joins and communicates with us through our spirits. From the time you and I were saved, in that very moment, the Holy Spirit came to dwell with our spirits.

We Must be Born of Water and of the Spirit

Jesus explained this beautifully. In the beginning of John chapter 3, we see Nicodemus coming to talk to Jesus. From the context of the story, we can tell it is kind of late in the evening. And, being a Head Honcho, Nicodemus didn't want people seeing him. So, he slipped in under cover of darkness:

> *3 There was a man of the Pharisees, named Nicodemus, a ruler of the Jews:*
>
> *2 The same came to Jesus by night, and said unto him, Rabbi, we know that thou art a teacher come from God: for no man can do these miracles that thou doest, except God be with him.*
>
> *3 Jesus answered and said unto him, Verily, verily, I say unto thee, **Except a man be born again**[62], he cannot see the kingdom of God.*
>
> *4 Nicodemus saith unto him, How can a man be born when he is old? Can he enter the second time into his mother's womb, and be born?*
>
> *5 Jesus answered, Verily, verily, I say unto thee, **Except a man be born of water and of the Spirit**, he cannot enter into the kingdom of God.*
>
> *6 **That which is born of the flesh is flesh; and that which is born of the Spirit is spirit.** (John 3:1-6, KJV,* emphasis added – footnote at verse three added*)*

What does Jesus mean when He says, "*Except a man be born of water...,*" in verse five? Look carefully at the verse. It says

[62] Jesus answered him, "I assure you *and* most solemnly say to you, unless a person is born again [**reborn from above—spiritually transformed, renewed, sanctified**], he cannot [ever] see *and* experience the kingdom of God." (John 3:3, AMP. emphasis added)

unless a man is born of water *and* of the Spirit, so that means the water birth he's talking about is natural birth not baptism in water. Let me give you an additional scriptural witness before we move on:

> *25 Husbands, love your wives, even as Christ also loved the church, and gave himself for it;*
>
> *26 That he might sanctify and cleanse it* **with the washing of water by the word,** *(Ephesians 5:25-26, KJV, emphasis added)*

Now, in my Bible, when I look in the margin where it says, *"with the washing of water by the word,"* it gives reference to John 3:5. I am in full agreement with water baptism. It's a doctrine of the Church. Jesus himself practiced it, and we should too. But you must understand, water baptism never saved anyone spiritually.

Being born of the water can't save people. Yet some people will still emphasize, "Well, you know I was baptized in water on this date." I watch them and I'm not sure they're saved. They think being baptized, or born of water, saved them because of a misinterpretation of this Bible verse. Unfortunately, that's not what it is talking about. This verse is talking about the natural birth.

I want to stress again, I do believe in water baptism because it is a doctrine of the Church. But it should only be done *after* a confession of faith in Jesus Christ is made. Then the Blood has already come and cleansed them spiritually.

Jesus went on to further explain it in John 3:6, when He said you and I have two birthdays: a physical birthday and a spiritual birthday. Remember, when you and I were born of the Spirit, that's when the Holy Ghost came into our heart and joined with our newly reborn spirit. Jesus, Himself, confirms the Holy Ghost is neither joined with our mind nor is He joined with our

84

body. He's joined with our spirit because, *"...that which is born of the Spirit is spirit."*

Don't misunderstand me, the Holy Spirit dwells within us, and as long as we live in our body, He's going to be in our body. But, once our spirit leaves our body and leaves Planet Earth, the Holy Ghost leaves too. He will not stay in that dead body, because He lives in our spirit and goes wherever we go[63].

Hollywood likes to portray dead people still wandering around searching for something. I don't care what Hollywood portrays – that's not scriptural! God said when *you* leave your body, *you* have left. So, we want to make sure that we teach people to realize who they are in Christ, their place in the Body of Christ, and what belongs to them as children of God. We don't want anyone to be tricked into believing things that aren't true, because then the devil can waltz right in and steal the victory from them. Christians should live victoriously because that's what God wants for His children.

---

63 John 14:12-17

Chapter 8 – Eternal Life and the Divine Nature

Every human being has an eternal spirit – a spirit that is designed to live forever once the physical body dies and decays. All of humanity was originally designed to live forever with God. After the fall, that was no longer possible until Jesus came as a sacrifice for our sins. Now, every human spirit has two choices, we can accept Jesus' offer of salvation and spend eternity with Him in Glory, or, we can reject it and spend eternity in hell which was created for Satan and his army.

So the true question isn't really how long your spirit will live, rather ask yourself:

1. Which spirit nature do I have right now?

2. Where will my spirit man spend eternity when I leave my earthsuit behind?

3. How victoriously do I want to live while I am here on Earth?

At the time we were born again spiritually and the Holy Spirit came into our lives, the very life and nature of God was supernaturally imparted into each of our newly reborn spirits. (If you aren't sure you have ever been born again spiritually, I urge you to turn to Appendix 1 and take care of that right now. It is very simple. Don't wait. None of us is guaranteed tomorrow.)

Eternal Life – More than Life as You Know It

> *23 For the wages of sin is death; but **the gift of God is eternal life** through Jesus Christ our Lord. (Romans 6:23, KJV, emphasis added)*

The gift mentioned in Romans 6:23, supernaturally imparted into our newly reborn spirit at salvation, is eternal life and a ticket to live with Jesus in Heaven for the rest of eternity. But it is more than just a longer version of life as we know it here and now. *It is the very life, nature, and character of our unchanging God for eternity.* In fact, all nine Fruit of the Spirit were imparted into our newly reborn spirit – they came with the Holy Ghost and they are each a facet of God's Divine Nature[64].

The fifth chapter of John gives New Testament proof of this. Everything God the Father had, meaning all nine Fruit of the Spirit, He gave to Jesus so Jesus could give it to us.

> *26 For as **the Father hath life in himself**; so hath he given to the Son to have life in himself; (John 5:26, KJV, emphasis added)*

For more clarity, let's also look at this verse in the New Living Translation:

> *26 The Father has life in himself, and he has granted that same life-giving power to his Son. (John 5:26, NLT)*

---

64 Galatians 5:22-23 (love, joy, peace, patience, kindness, goodness, faithfulness, gentleness, and self-control)

Now, that word "life" in both of these translations is the word "Zoë" in the original Greek (Interlinear Bible)[65]. It means the very life and nature of God – the *way* He lives not just how long He lives.

The abundant life that John and Paul both wrote about is Divine Nature of God. Peter is another witness in the New Testament about us receiving God's Divine Nature.

> *4 Whereby are **given unto us exceeding great and precious promises**: that by these ye might be partakers of **the divine nature**, having escaped the corruption that is in the world through lust. (2 Peter 1:4, KJV, emphasis added)*

At the time of being born again, God took the old spirit and nature of death[66] out of us and gave us a new spirit[67]. Our *new spirit* has the life and nature of God in it. This reminds me of an old worship song that goes something like this:

I've got the life of God in me.
I've got the life of God in me.
I've got his love, his nature and his ability.
I've got the life of God in me[68].

---

[65] For more information on the Zoë life of God, see Brother Hagin's book titled *"Zoe: The God-Kind of Life."*

[66] John 5:24 and 1 John 3:14

[67] 2 Corinthians 5:17

[68] http://www.traditionalmusic.co.uk/gospel-praise-chords/ive_got_the_life_of_go_in_me.html

So, if you've got the Divine Nature in you, where is it located? It is in your spirit, because God is Spirit[69]. So, if God's Spirit is in your spirit then that makes your spirit right with God and everything that God has in His Spirit, you have in yours. That's why Peter says, *"...that by these ye might be partakers of the Divine Nature, having escaped the corruption that is in the world through lust."* Your spirit cannot be corrupted because it is partaking of, or joined with, God's Spirit.

When Paul mentions the great and precious promises that we have been given, he's talking about everything that belongs to us as children of God – everything that salvation has given us a right to access. I've said it before, but it bears repeating, if you don't know what belongs to you, it won't matter that you have the Divine Nature of God in you – you will still live a defeated life. This means a Christian can still give way to habits and different things that unsaved people do. But, just because a Christian struggles in some areas doesn't mean he isn't born again.

Don't Just Qualify – Go on to Receive

The life that God gave Jesus is the same life He gives to each of us when we are born again spiritually. But it's not in your mind or in your body. It's in you – the real you – you're spirit man. Getting saved spiritually is only the beginning. It only *qualifies* you as a child of God for a home in Heaven and certain privileges on Earth. You *receive* the privileges when you find out about them by renewing your mind with the WORD and act upon them by faith. Therefore, if you never renew your mind to what's yours as a child of the Most High God, you'll be doomed to struggle along living by your lower nature, being held hostage by your flesh and

69

soul, and acting as if you were never saved, rather than partaking of His Divine Nature and all the rights and privileges thereof. That's why Paul warned the Church at Ephesus to stop walking like Gentiles or those without a covenant:

> *[17] This I say therefore, and testify in the Lord, that ye henceforth walk not as other Gentiles walk, in the vanity of their mind,*
>
> *[18] Having the understanding darkened, being alienated from the life of God through the ignorance that is in them, because of the blindness of their heart: (Ephesians 4:17-18, KJV)*

When we look at this Scripture passage in a modern translation, it is even more striking how important it is to keep the mind renewed:

> *[17] With the Lord's authority I say this: Live no longer as the Gentiles do, for they are hopelessly confused. [18] Their minds are full of darkness; they wander far from the life God gives because they have closed their minds and hardened their hearts against him. (Ephesians 4:17-18, NLT)*

The prophet Ezekiel got a revelation of this. That's why he wrote that God will take the stony heart out of you and give you a heart of flesh[70]. Even Ezekiel saw it and longed for it. The Bible says the prophets of old saw over into the Church Age. They didn't get to be partakers of it, but they were like, "Oh, we'd sure like to live over there[71]!"

---

[70] Ezekiel 36:26

[71] Look at Hebrews 11 for more patriarchs who saw what God was doing by faith.

Isn't it amazing, a lot of Christians today want to go back to the Old Covenant? Yet everyone under the Old Covenant kept looking ahead saying, "None of us get to be saved by grace, but look at that group out there. They don't have to be servants of God – they get to be *children* of God!" Aren't you glad we are in a better covenant[72]?

Drawing on the Benefits of the Divine Nature Within You

As you start to truly understand what it means to have God's Spirit and Divine Nature inside you dwelling in your spirit, you'll start to see the benefits manifesting in your own life. Paul wrote about this in Romans 8.

> But if the Spirit of him that raised up Jesus from the dead dwell in you, he that raised up Christ from the dead shall also quicken your mortal bodies by his Spirit that dwelleth in you. (Romans 8:11, KJV).

So as you get older, when anything that's in your human body (e.g., heart, pancreas, liver, etc.) begins to die, if you learn to tap into the life of God inside you, it will quicken or revive it. This brings to mind a story Brother Hagin used to tell us about his own life when we were at Rhema:

One time he fell and was having a heart attack. Two ministers were with him and picked him up and laid him on a table. They couldn't get a strong heart beat. It was more like a flutter. Sister Oretha, his wife, was in another part of the church. She knew by the Holy Ghost something was going on and she came

---

bursting through the door about the same time, they laid him on the table. She and Brother Hagin prayed together and he was raised up.

Now, when he told us about this, he specifically said, "It was the life of God on the inside of me that literally picked me up off that table and put me on my feet." This is very important to understand. Healing is available to both the church and the world. But divine health is available *only* to the church.

Now, remember, Romans 8:11 says, *"The Spirit of God, who raised Jesus from the dead, lives in you. And just as God raised Christ Jesus from the dead, he will give life to your mortal bodies by this same Spirit living within you" (NLT).* Brother Hagin would tell us, "I've learned how to tap into divine health."

This is what I'm going after as well. It has to do with tapping in to the life of God that Jesus came and deposited in us when we got saved. Remember, He told us in John 10:10, that He, *"...came that they may have and enjoy life, and have it in abundance (to the full, till it overflows)" (John 10:10b, Amplified Bible, Classic Edition "AMPC").* I'm after the overflowing life of God in me.

It's happening too. I have life insurance policies because of real estate stuff that we do. Every year, the banks require me to go and get a policy. For the last few years, I noticed the insurance companies have been putting on the form, "One healthy individual."

I got tickled about it and thought, "Only in Pawnee, Oklahoma." Then one day, I was having my hearing and vision checked. The lady had this machine and she was going to put it to my ear. It was supposed to make a high pitched noise. But it wouldn't work. So she said, "OK, I tell you what I'll do. I'm going to walk 20 feet down the hall and then I'm going to whisper and you tell me when you can hear me."

Again I thought, "Only in Pawnee!"

So, she went down the hall 20 feet and whispered, "Can you hear me?" and I told her I could.

"Yep, you can hear all right," she said quite matter-of-factly.

You see when I was 25, because I drank so much and did so many drugs, I wasn't as healthy as I am today – especially in my organs. I had back trouble, knee trouble, and some trouble in my belly because I got run over in a stampede one time. I had horseshoe prints all over me. But, I don't have that any more. Praise God! See, I'm learning to tap into the life of God, and it's affecting my mortal body. We're all getting older, and the body we live in is getting older, but it ought to last as long as we need it. If we'll learn to tap into the life of God inside us, it will.

Consequences of Ignoring the Divine Nature Within You

Not only will the Spirit living inside us quicken us in our physical bodies, and make our spirits alive in Christ, but it will also lead us as children of God[73]. This is why it is so important for us to learn how to live from the inside out. We must learn to live with our spirit man leading the way, because that is the part that is joined with the Holy Ghost. The Spirit of God inside us will guide, constrain, and keep us. The Divine Nature of God will flow through us. But in order to live this way, from the inside out, we

---

73 Romans 8:14

must keep our minds renewed every day. Otherwise they will take us places we really have no business going.

I had an Aunt who was a perfect example of this. Her name was Ruth. She and my Uncle lived on 40 acres near us in Oklahoma. One time, we stopped in to visit her. She was crying and all upset. My dad asked her what was wrong. She told him some lady had died. I was young and don't really remember the lady's name, so for our purposes, we'll just use the name Bertha.

Anyway, Aunt Ruth was all upset about this Miss Bertha dying. I mean she was torn up. I'd never seen anything like it. Well, as she was relating the story to my dad, we eventually found out this woman was a character on Days of Our Lives[74]! She got so tangled up that she could no longer tell fantasy from reality. Her mind took her places she had no business going – oh LORD!

Now, here's the thing, I believe Aunt Ruth was saved. I believe she made Heaven when she died. But victory? Nope. None. She was crippled. She wasn't that old. She was tangled up with arthritis and had begun to have all kinds of mental trouble. I have no doubt she was a child of God. But she looked just like the beggar Lazarus in Luke 16 that died sick and broke even though he had a Covenant promising him prosperity and health.

I believe if Aunt Ruth had spent as much time with the WORD of God as she did with the silly soap opera she would have learned about the Divine Nature within her and things would have been different. She would have seen some victory in her life. So many people make the mistake of believing all they have to do is get saved and everything else will take care of itself. Then when it doesn't, they don't understand what is happening. This opens the

---

[74] Days of Our Lives is NBC's longest running daytime drama (aka soap opera). It debuted in 1965 and still runs today. (Days of Our Lives)

door to discouragement and other wrong thinking. Once wrong thinking of any kind is allowed in, the devil can just come right in and have a heyday.

Chapter 9 – Sin Affects the Soul Not the Spirit

Right Spirit vs. Right Soul

King David, in the Old Testament, was the second king of Israel and lived under the Old Covenant with God[75]. The Old Testament is full of types and shadows, or pictures, of things to come under the New Covenant which Jesus would establish after His death, burial, and resurrection. David longed for the things that he saw coming under the New Covenant, so he wrote:

> *[10] Create in me a clean heart, O God;*
> *and renew a right spirit within me.*
> *(Psalm 51:10, KJV)*

In Psalm 51:10, David prayed and asked God to create a clean heart and right spirit within him, because he couldn't be born again or saved by grace. Why not? Because Jesus hadn't died on the cross and been resurrected yet. Nobody under the Old Covenant could be saved spiritually. Therefore, David's prayer was scripturally correct at that time.

But that same prayer is no longer scripturally correct for modern Christians, because we are completely new creations according to 2 Corinthians 5:17. Remember it tells us, at the time we became born again, *"...old things are passed away; behold all things become new" (KJV).* That means we took on the life and

---

[75]The Old Covenant is often referred to as "The Law" but it is really much more than that name implies. You can read about it in Exodus chapters 19-24.

nature of God in our born again human spirit at salvation. In other words, we have a completely clean heart that is brand new and perfectly right with God because it is just like God's!

Now, I know there is a hymn along these same lines with a verse, "Create in me, O God, a clean heart and right spirit,[76]" but what they are really meaning in that hymn is, "LORD, I really don't want to do this bad stuff, but I keep finding myself doing it. So, LORD, please create a clean *soul* in me." You see those people, even though they have been saved, don't fully understand that their reborn spirit man doesn't sin. They get confused because everyone's soul and flesh can mess up and wreak all kinds of havoc in their life and the lives of others. When this is going on, it doesn't mean they aren't saved, it just shows that their soul hasn't been saved, or lined up with their spirit yet. The only way to do that is by the renewing of the mind with the WORD.

Let's dig into this a little deeper to understand it better.

> [5] *And ye know that* ***he was manifested to take away our sins;*** *and* ***in him is no sin.***
>
> [6] *Whosoever abideth in him sinneth not: whosoever sinneth hath not seen him, neither known him.*
>
> [7] *Little children, let no man deceive you: he that doeth righteousness is righteous, even as he is righteous.*
>
> [8] ***He that committeth sin is of the devil; for the devil sinneth from the beginning.*** *For this purpose the Son of God was manifested, that he might destroy the works of the devil.*

---

[76] Composed by J.A. Freylinghausen, 1670-1739

> [9] *Whosoever is born of God doth not commit sin; for his seed remaineth in him: and he cannot sin, because he is born of God. (1 John 3:5-9, KJV, emphasis added)*

Everybody, even after they've been saved spiritually and filled with the Holy Ghost, will yield to their soul or their flesh and sin. For example, I bet you've probably gotten angry in traffic or gossiped about someone within the last six months. Is that sin? Yes, of course it is[77]. We've all done it. We've all sinned after we were born again. We aren't just floating around down here with halos on. We have to be real honest about this stuff if we are going to get victory over it.

One time, Brother Hagin was teaching on this and a guy came up to him and said, "Brother Hagin, you're just giving people a license to sin with this."

To which he responded, "I promise you, they don't need a license."

Worry won't keep you out of Heaven, but it sure will hurt your body. Drinking won't send you to hell either, but it sure can cost you a lot. The only thing that sends you to hell is not having Jesus in your life. Remember, once we're saved, sin cannot keep us out of Heaven, but it can keep us from experiencing everything God has for us.

Listen carefully here, don't run out and say, "Whoo-hoo, let's go burn our reefer 'cause the Pastor said ain't nobody going to hell around here!" That's not what I said! Besides that, it's not

---

[77] Ephesians 4:26, and Romans 1:29-32

legal in most states anyway. God's grace is never a license to give in to your flesh[78].

People get confused, because the Old English of the King James trips them up. We don't talk like that today, so you have to dig around to really understand the vocabulary. For example, according to the Interlinear Bible, that word "committeth" in verse eight actually means "practicing" in the original Greek. Let's look at this same section of Scripture in the Amplified Classic Version for more clarity.

> [8] *[But] he who commits sin [who practices evildoing] is of the devil [takes his character from the evil one], for the devil has sinned (violated the divine law) from the beginning. The reason the Son of God was made manifest (visible) was to undo (destroy, loosen, and dissolve) the works the devil [has done].*
>
> [9] *No one born (begotten) of God [deliberately, knowingly, and habitually] practices sin, for God's nature abides in him [His principle of life, the divine sperm, remains permanently within him]; and he cannot practice sinning because he is born (begotten) of God. (1 John 3:8-9, AMPC)*

Remember, when your soul is not saved and renewed by the WORD of God, it is going to join in with the flesh and the two of them will hold your spirit man hostage to do whatever they want to do. They will hold you in the carnal arena and cause you to continue sinning – even when your spirit man longs to stop. The flesh will hold you – the real you – captive.

---

[78] Romans 6:15-17

But if you can get your mind renewed with the WORD and get your soul saved, then the flesh has got another thing coming! Suddenly, the tables are turned and your soul will join forces with your spirit man and you – the real you – will take your flesh and hold it captive to do what God wants.

Now, look again at those verses in the KJV, *"...He that practices sin is of the devil; for the devil sinneth from the beginning...whosoever is born of God doth not commit sin; for his seed remaineth in him, and he cannot sin..."* Let me ask you this, what part of man is unable to sin? If he is born again, then his spirit man is unable to sin. Why is that? Because God's life is in them and God does not sin[79]. You see, when a Christian sins, if we could take an x-ray machine and look down inside them, we would see that their born again spirit didn't want to do that.

So, today, our spirits are clean before the LORD. We don't need to pray and ask Him to create a right spirit in us. It's a great prayer when we are struggling in an area of the soul, however, because He will guide us toward renewing our minds so we won't struggle in that area any longer. David longed for that type of relationship with God, because it wasn't yet available to mankind at the time he lived. He could only see it coming from afar off.

Dying to Self vs. Renewing the Soul

Along these same lines, have you ever heard someone say, "Well, I'm just dying to self," because they believe in self-denial? Here's the thing, you don't need to die to yourself, your true self that is, after spiritual salvation. However, you will have to do something with your soul and your body. We've been discussing

---

[79] James 1:13, Numbers 23:19, 2 Corinthians 5:21, 1 John 3:5

that you're going to have to renew your soul, but that's not all, you also have to keep your body under control. Paul informed us of this in 1 Corinthians 9:27. Here's an illustration I think many can relate to:

Some of us, before we got saved, used to fight people. Sometimes it wouldn't take much to set us off and we'd just deck them one. But, as we renewed our mind, we learned to handle things differently.

Yet, sometimes, we get tired or lazy about studying the WORD and praying in other tongues. Eventually, we start running on empty spiritually speaking. If someone comes up and slaps us when we are in that empty state, what is our body's first reaction? Some of us are going to physically slap them right back and *then* try to apologize!

However, if our soul has been full of the WORD and is in conjunction with our spirit man, then we'll have a different outcome. Our body might flash an idea to do something, but before our mind grabs it, our spirit will stop everything. Instead of hitting them back, we'll ask, "Why did you do that?"

> *Among whom also we all had our conversation in times past in the lusts of our flesh, fulfilling the desires of the flesh and of the mind; and were **by nature the children of wrath**, even as others.* (Ephesians 2:3, KJV, emphasis added)

Now, for a little more clarity, let's look at the Weymouth New Testament in Modern Speech ("WNT") for Ephesians 2:3:

> *Among them all of us also formerly passed our lives, **governed by the inclinations of our lower natures**, indulging the cravings of those natures*

> *and of our own thoughts, and were in*
> *our original state deserving of anger*
> *like all others. (Ephesians 2:3, WNT,*
> *emphasis added)*

When comparing translations of Ephesians 2:3, we see the King James says that we were, *"...by nature the children of wrath..."* The Weymouth translation calls this the "lower nature". Say out loud, "I don't live by my lower nature."

So, when people say, "I need to die to self," it shows they don't truly understand who "self" is. Because when you are born again, your true self is spiritually alive and you don't need to die to that. You are fine. But the lower nature is the flesh, and if the soul has never been saved, it will join forces with the flesh to take control. We don't want to be carnal bottom dwellers!

Carnality Blocks Spiritual Understanding and Opens the Door to the Enemy

Remember I shared with you how the word "heart" in Scripture usually refers to a person's core being or spirit man, but sometimes it refers to the soul. We see this again in Ephesians 4:23 as Paul uses the word "spirit" to refer to the soul.

> *23 And be renewed **in the spirit of your***
> ***mind;** (Ephesians 4:23, KJV, emphasis*
> *added)*

We know he couldn't have been referring to the core being or spirit man, because once you are saved there is no renewing the spirit man. At salvation, the spirit is as good as it gets, because it was born anew and made right with God. Additionally, when you read carefully, you see the word "spirit" is associated with the mind in this verse. We know that the mind is part of the soul. So, from that, we understand that he's talking about the mind, the will, and the emotions of a man and not the human spirit[80].

This brings up an important point about the mind that needs to be discussed. It is one that causes much confusion in the Body of Christ. Back in the late 80s, there were great debates and discussions about whether Christians could be demon possessed or not. We all need to understand this – a Christian can never be *possessed* by a devil because *the Holy Ghost lives in his spirit*. Think about it, if the Holy Ghost lives there, then it must be *right* or God Himself wouldn't be residing there. However, a Christian can be *oppressed* in their soul or in their body by an evil spirit who has established a stronghold. But even so, that doesn't mean they can be completely taken over by them.

Many of you have known people who have been saved and they've lost their mind. I've known some. Well, if they were right spiritually with God before they lost their mind, they're headed to Heaven. We lost our parents to cancer, but I know beyond a shadow of a doubt that Mom and Dad are both in Glory. They loved God with all their heart, they were born again, and spirit filled. It is no different with a mental illness – it is not demon possession and you don't lose your salvation just because you lose your mind.

In Romans 8, Paul is writing to the Church at Rome and he makes this statement that I find very interesting:

> [6] *For to be **carnally minded is death**; but to be **spiritually minded is life and peace**.*

---

[80] Remember, when you read the Bible you have to always *READ* the Bible carefully – don't just gloss over it like a novel.

> [7] Because **the carnal mind is enmity**
> **against God**: for it is not subject to **the**
> **law of God**[81], neither indeed can be.
> *(Romans 8:6-7, KJV, emphasis added, footnote*
> *mine)*

If you have a reference Bible of any sort, you probably have a note at Romans 8:6 to explain that the original Greek of "... *to be carnally minded is death...*" meant "the minding of the flesh is death" (Interlinear Bible). In today's language, one definition would be, "For the mind to be controlled by the old nature – still subject to sense and reason."

So, according to verse seven, the carnal mind will fight God. A perfect example of this is when we are mad and someone tries to talk to us about the situation. We can't receive anything because we're so mad. At that moment, we're shut off from taking in anything, because our carnal mind is in control. There was a time, when I was in that state, I'd say, "Don't talk to me right now. I ain't listening to a word you're saying."

When our carnal mind is in control, not only are we shut off from taking anything in, but we also open up the door to receiving things we don't want. Brother Hagin made the statement, "Usually sickness will come through an unrenewed mind which gives way to the flesh." I find the same thing is true with most financial problems too. Yet, when you try to tell someone that is sick or struggling with financial problems that Jesus provided healing or prosperity for them, their unrenewed mind will fight you.

Another example of this is when people say, "Well, then, how do you know all this stuff is right?" They're meaning the things in the Bible when they ask me that. I believe it because it's

---

[81] The law of God is the WORD of God.

in the WORD of God. Believing because it's in the WORD of God is called FAITH. Let's take a look at the Law of Faith:

> *So then **faith cometh by hearing**, and hearing by the word of God. (Romans 10:17, KJV, emphasis added)*

The faith that comes to you by hearing the WORD of God is established in your heart.

> *⁹ That if thou shalt **confess with thy mouth** the Lord Jesus, and shalt **believe in thine heart** that God hath raised him from the dead, thou shalt be saved.*
>
> *¹⁰ For with the heart man believeth unto righteousness; and with the mouth confession is made unto salvation. (Romans 10:9-10, KJV, emphasis added)*

Now, Romans 10 is telling us if you believe in your heart and confess with your mouth you will be saved. So, this means faith has got to be in two places – in our heart but also in our mouth. To believe God, we must believe Him with our heart first. Then, as we renew our mind to His WORD, what's in our heart will start to overflow out of our mouth and change the circumstances around us.

Before we move on, let's take a moment and review with a little quiz to make sure this is crystal clear (*the answers are in the footnotes if you aren't sure*):

1. What part of you and I got saved when we asked Jesus into our lives? [82]

2. So spiritually, we were made what? [83]

---

[82] Our spirit man.

[83] Brand new.

3. Did our soul get saved at that time? [84]

4. What do we have to do with the soul? [85]

5. If our soul is not saved or renewed with the WORD of God, it will side in with what? [86]

Again, if someone's body is screaming, "I'm tired...I'm hungry...I don't like them...dah, dah, dah," and their soul hasn't been renewed with the WORD, then their soul will side in with the flesh. Then the soul and flesh will dictate to a Christian to think and act that way towards others. I'm not exactly sure when or why the Church, as a whole, ever thought their soul got saved when their spirit did, but this error has caused many Christians to struggle along unnecessarily in defeat for far too long.

---

[84] No.

[85] Renew it with the WORD of God.

[86] The flesh, thereby allowing the enemy into a Christian's life.

Chapter 10 – Born of Water – Cleansed by the Blood – Washed with The WORD

The Blood for the Spirit – The WORD for the Soul

Remember in John 3:5 Jesus told Nicodemus, *"Except a man be born of water..." (KJV)*. Always remember, being born of water isn't the same as being baptized in water. The scripture says unless a man is born of water *and* born of the spirit. Getting spiritually saved makes us ready for Heaven, but that, in and of itself, doesn't make us victorious on Planet Earth. Really and truly it just makes you more of a target for the enemy now than ever before. Why is that? Because Satan hates God and God's children. Therefore, if you're not taught who you are in Christ, then you'll just go from disaster to disaster instead of from victory to victory.

I believe everyone reading this book will agree with me that the word "washing" means to cleanse or to make clean. In Ephesians 5:25-26, Paul talks about Christ's love for us being so strong that He gave Himself up so, *"That he might sanctify and cleanse us with the washing of water by The Word" (v. 26 KJV)*.

Can the washing with the water of the WORD save you? No, only the Blood of Jesus can save you and wash your spirit. Furthermore, the Blood of Jesus bought you spiritually, but it doesn't wash your soul. So, you (the real you — the spirit man) is cleansed spiritually by the Blood when you're saved. But, the only way to get your soul (your mind, your will, and your emotions) cleansed is to wash it with the WORD.

> *23 For all have sinned, and come short of the glory of God;*
>
> *24 Being justified freely by his grace through the redemption that is in Christ Jesus:*
>
> *25 Whom God hath set forth to be a propitiation through faith in his blood, to declare his righteousness for the remission of sins that are past, through the forbearance of God; (Romans 3:23, KJV)*

It took the Blood of God that flowed through Jesus' veins to be poured out to cleanse you and I spiritually. That's why we have faith in the Blood. When we were born again and washed by the Blood spiritually, instantly we were made right with God. In 2 Corinthians 5:17-18, Paul talked about how we were made new creatures and were then given the ministry of reconciliation:

> *17 Therefore if any man be in Christ, he is a new creature: old things are passed away; behold, all things are become new.*
>
> *18 And all things are of God, who hath reconciled us to himself by Jesus Christ, and hath given to us the ministry of reconciliation; (2 Corinthians 5:17-18, KJV)*
>
> *21 For he hath made him to be sin for us, who knew no sin; that we might be made the **righteousness** of God in him. (2 Corinthians 5:21, KJV, emphasis added)*

That word "righteousness" means right standing. We used to think, but we don't any more, that we were old sinners saved by grace. Thank God! We now understand the correct terminology is that we are the righteousness of God in Christ Jesus. I'm not an old sinner saved by grace. I'm talking about my spirit man – the real me – the part that was made right at salvation. Instantly, I was put in right standing with God, because I have faith in the Blood of Jesus.

> *Neither by the blood of goats and calves, but by his own blood he entered in once into the holy place, having obtained eternal redemption for us. (Hebrews 9:12, KJV)*

It took the Blood to wash and cleanse us spiritually so we could be saved. But it takes the washing of the water of the WORD to save our souls. Let me say that again. It takes the washing of the water by the WORD to save our souls, but it took the Blood of Jesus to cleanse us and save us spiritually.

In spiritual salvation, everything is forgiven and forgotten. It's over and it's under the Blood because we were made right with God. The only place the enemy can usually then beat up a Christian is through their soul. But if you will get your soul saved by the renewing of the mind with the WORD of God, then it's not going to accept those crazy thoughts coming. Instead, it will agree with the spirit man that you are the righteousness of God in Christ Jesus.

At that point, you are in a position to better understand your rights and privileges as a child of God. You won't feel like a cowed down person. Instead, you'll feel worthy. You aren't worthy because you're so wonderful, but because Jesus died for you. Once you understand that, you'll start to go after some things because you know you are right with God.

A person told me several times, "We used to think you were such an arrogant guy because you were just so confident."

I replied, "My confidence ain't in Ricky. I know what Ricky used to be before I got saved, and I was a mess!" I've learned if it's good – it's God. It took the Blood to put me in right standing with God spiritually, but it takes the WORD being infused through my soul daily to put me in right thinking with where I am spiritually.

Discerning the Body of Christ

In addition to understanding the relationship between sin and the believer, we need to properly understand the relationship between Jesus and the Body of Christ, in order to fully walk in everything God has planned for us.

> [18] *And he is **the head of the body, the church**: who is the beginning, **the firstborn from the dead**; that in all things he might have the preeminence.* (Colossians 1:18, KJV, emphasis added)

According to Colossians 1:18, Jesus was the firstborn from the dead. That means He was the first one to ever be raised from the dead spiritually. Let me ask you this, have you ever wondered why it had to be Jesus? Well, it's because He was the only begotten Son of God.

In Genesis 22, Abraham and Isaac went up on Mt. Moriah. Abraham was going to sacrifice Isaac. He was about to jab a knife in the boy when God said, "Abraham, do the lad no harm" (vs. 1-19). Why didn't God allow Abraham to go ahead and sacrifice him? Because Isaac was just like you and I. His blood wouldn't have qualified because it wasn't sinless and pure. That's why Jesus had to come.

Mary was the true mother of Jesus, but Joseph wasn't his daddy. Jesus did not have the fallen nature in him. He was the sinless, spotless Lamb of God. Jesus never sinned, but he took our sin. He was the Lamb of God. That's why John said what he did when Jesus came over to the banks of the Jordan. Imagine it. John is down there baptizing folks, suddenly he looks up says, "Behold, the Lamb of God![87]"

Well, everybody there that day who studied the Old Testament ought to have immediately understood he was saying that Jesus was the Messiah – the One they had all been looking for. Since He was sinless, as soon as Jesus died and rose again on the third day, He became the first begotten from the dead.

We are complete in Jesus because in Him is the fullness[88]. Look at verse 18 again, *"He is the head of the body of the church."* Now, remember, when Jesus was here on Planet Earth, He was the *physical* body of Christ. When He died spiritually, and physically, and rose from the dead, He was no longer the *physical* body of Christ. Instead, He became, according to this verse, the *spiritual* Head. Now, we, the Church, all make up the *spiritual* Body of Christ. Jesus is the *spiritual* Head, and we're the *spiritual* Body.

Colossians 1:18 also goes on to say that Jesus was the firstborn or first begotten of the dead. So, this means that Jesus was the very first person die and rise up again *spiritually*. There's been a whole bunch of us since Him, but Jesus was the first. David and the prophets longed for it, but Jesus was the first.

> [23] *For I have received of the Lord that*
> *which also I delivered unto you, that the*
> *Lord Jesus the same night in which he*

---

[87] John 1:29

[88] Colossians 2:9

was betrayed took bread: (1 Corinthians 11:23, KJV)

In 1 Corinthians 11:23, Paul is writing to the Church of Corinth. To put it in today's language, Paul was saying, "What I'm going to tell you, I wasn't taught by man. Instead, Jesus, Himself, told me. For I have received what I'm going to tell you directly from The LORD." If you have a red-letter edition of the Bible, you'll see the next two verses, 24 and 25, are in red. That means Jesus told Paul directly. Now, if Jesus told him directly, it also means Jesus must have appeared to him. That means Jesus put great emphasis on this!

Most of us have a full-time job just keeping after ourselves. But many Christians don't realize just how important this is.

> 28 *But let a man examine himself, and so let him eat of that bread, and drink of that cup.*
>
> 29 *For he that eateth and drinketh unworthily, eateth and drinketh damnation to himself, not discerning the Lord's body. (1 Corinthians 11:28-29, KJV)*

Let's review for a moment before digging into the next layer. When Jesus was here, was He the *body of Christ*? Yes! When He died and rose from the dead, what did He become? The Head of the Body. Then who makes up the Body now? The Church.

In this, we see that if we don't understand what Jesus has done for us when He was the *body of Christ*, then according to 1 Corinthians 11:29, we will have some difficulty in our life. God has provided everything I need to live victoriously. Yet, if I don't understand exactly what Jesus did for me when He was the *body*, then I can be saved, have Jesus as my LORD, and still miss one

side of it because I don't discern and understand what Jesus died
for.

> *19 For the good that I would I do not: but
> the evil which I would not, that I do.*
>
> *20 Now if I do that I would not, it is no
> more I that do it, but sin that dwelleth in
> me.*
>
> *21 I find then a law, that, when I would
> do good, evil is present with me.*
>
> *22 For I delight in the law of God after
> the inward man:*
>
> *23 But I see another law in my members,
> warring against the law of my mind, and
> bringing me into captivity to the law of
> sin which is in my members.*
>
> *24 O wretched man that I am! who shall
> deliver me from the body of this death?*
>
> *25 I thank God through Jesus Christ our
> Lord. So then with the mind I myself
> serve the law of God; but with the flesh
> the law of sin. (Romans 7:19-25, KJV,
> emphasis added)*

In Romans 7:19-25, the members Paul is talking about are
our body parts – eyes, ears, hands, tongue – the members of our
body.

Let's turn the page to Romans chapter 8.

> *There is therefore now no condemnation
> to them which are in Christ Jesus, who
> walk not after the flesh, but after the
> Spirit. (Romans 8:1, KJV)*

In Romans 7, Paul was talking about how he was alive once
without the Law, but when the Law came sin revived and he died.
Now, when he says he died, he means his spirit man died. We

know this because of Adam and Eve in the Garden of Eden. When God told Adam and Eve if they ate of that tree they would die, He meant they would die spiritually not physically. Paul is referring to the same thing. You see, before a child reaches the age of accountability, they are spiritually alive unto God. Eventually, when the day of accountability comes, if they've been taught who Jesus is by the WORD, they'll just make the transition and accept Jesus as LORD. If not, their spirit dies.

Paul said that he was alive without the Law, but when the Law came and revealed how to live, at the age of accountability, he died spiritually. Prior to understanding the Law, he said he couldn't figure out what was going on, "O wretched man that I am. I find myself doing and thinking 'the things I don't want to do, I do![89]'"

But he goes on to say, *"There is therefore now no condemnation to them which are in Christ Jesus..." (Romans 8:1, KJV).* He's talking about being saved, but first he had to find out that he was a spirit, that he had a soul, that he lived in a body, and that his soul needed to be saved. He needed to learn that if he left his soul unsaved and his mind unrenewed, then it was going to join forces with his flesh and lead him around even though his spirit was saved and made brand new. That meant he would keep on doing those things he didn't want to do until he got his soul saved.

Lack of Knowledge Breeds Carnality

I have a very dear friend, who is a Baptist preacher, named Bob Copeland. One time, he and I were discussing faith matters and he commented, "We put a heavy emphasis on getting people saved. That puts them into the kingdom. But, then, we don't teach

---

[89] Romans 7:15-24

them much beyond that. That's why they keep struggling." He meant that these fellow brothers and sisters in Christ continued to struggle with carnality because of a lack of knowledge. That's why many of them keep on with the same habits they had before salvation. Their souls aren't saved; therefore they cannot control their flesh.

Keep the main thing the main thing here, neither Pastor Bob nor I are saying that these Baptist men and women weren't saved. We both believe their salvations were genuine and they love God. There are carnal Christians in every denomination all over the world. Carnality is something that is common to all men if we don't learn to renew our mind and keep it renewed.

In fact, I know some Pentecostal folks that I would not go to a restaurant with because they are mean. They are very demanding and rude to the waitresses. When I see this, I think, "Dear God, where is the love of God at in you?"

You know the type – they can't control their carnal nature at all. The waitress will bring the rolls out and they'll snap, "Take these back they're cold!"

When that happens, if they're with me, I say, "Really? Would you not act that way when I'm with you? I live here. You might be visiting, but I live here. This is my town. I don't want them thinking I'm a nut or a carnal bucket like you are."

We don't want the lower nature to govern us. We want to govern it. Let's look at Ephesians 2:3 again:

> *3Among whom also we all had our conversation in times past in the lusts of our flesh, **fulfilling the desires of the flesh and of the mind**; and were by nature the children of wrath, even as*

others. *(Ephesians 2:3, KJV, emphasis added)*

Paul was writing to the born-again Christians at the Church of Ephesus. According to verse three, what happened to draw them to live by the lower nature? Remember, the soul is made up of the mind, the will, and the emotions. So we see here that they were, "...*fulfilling the desires of the flesh and of the mind....*" Therefore, we understand their souls were not saved — they were unrenewed and carnal. In other words, their soul had joined in with their flesh and was overriding the desires of their reborn spirit. The lower nature was governing them and they were basically running around acting like the rest of the unsaved folk.

God has given us everything we need for living a victorious, godly life and for governing our lower nature.

> *3 According as his divine power hath given unto us all things that pertain unto life and godliness, through the knowledge of him that hath called us to glory and virtue:*
>
> *4 Whereby are given unto us exceeding great and precious promises: that by these ye might be partakers of the divine nature, having escaped the corruption that is in the world through lust. (2 Peter 1:3-4, KJV, emphasis added)*

Aren't you glad there are promises given? They are precious and they are great! Study 2 Peter 1:4 carefully, especially the last half of it. Peter is telling us that, "...*by these promises we might be partakers of the Divine Nature...*" He's talking about the life and character of God that we discussed earlier in Chapter 1. Now focus on the phrase, "...*having escaped the corruption that is in the world through lust.*" Therefore, according to Ephesians 2:3, where is the lust going to filter through? First through an unrenewed or unsaved soul, and then through the flesh. Now, where is the Divine Nature? In our spirit-man.

Let's keep all of this straight. If you are saved and born-again, then your name is written in the *Lamb's Book of Life*, and there is a place prepared for you in Glory. But, at the same time, we don't want to leave here and go to Glory until we get through with everything God has planned for us. We want to live victoriously on Planet Earth. In order to do that, we have to keep our mind renewed with the WORD of God so we can govern our lower nature rather than it governing us and shortening our life or stealing our provision.

Boys Will be Boys

I remember a story Brother Kenneth Copeland shared in a Southwest Believer's Convention a few years ago about the time a rooster had him pinned on a trailer one Sunday when he was just a boy of about 12 or so. Now, he was born again but he wasn't at church with his momma because his dad, Mr. Copeland, wasn't attending at that time.

They had a neighbor and his neighbor seemed like a professional cusser and he had heard this neighbor cuss quite a bit. Since he was outside and his parents weren't around, Brother Copeland thought he'd try cussing this rooster out since he'd heard the neighbor do it so much. So he threw out a cuss word and then he froze waiting on lightning to strike him or something. He really thought something was going to happen. When nothing happened, he did it again, but he said two of them. After that, he said he just cussed a blue streak. Yet, he was born again and he knew it.

See you can cuss, be saved, be filled with the Spirit, and talk in tongues, and with an unrenewed mind it's not going to bother you much. However, if you'll listen when you act wrong, there'll be something down in your spirit that will scratch at you. It'll bother you if you'll listen to it, because we do have something on the inside of us to direct us – the Holy Spirit.

You know, when I get upset in traffic, I usually want to say something. Especially those times when my wife isn't with me, I'll hear the Holy Ghost speak up. And in my spirit, down here in the center of my gut where my heart is, I'll hear, "No, you don't want to do that."

But my body is screaming, "Oh yes I do! Yes I do!" With spiritual maturity, I've learned to listen to the Holy Ghost and not my body.

Chapter 11 – People, Places, and Things

My wife, Sally, and I came back into fellowship with God at the end of 1984. In this book, I've already testified that before I got saved, I was a drunk. I'm serious, as far as I can recall, I drank every day. I've further explained that once I got filled with the Holy Ghost, I discovered I no longer needed to be filled with alcohol.

Before we got saved, my wife and I used to love going into bars to play pool. In fact, we've been in some doozies. I mean, some of them were so bad we wouldn't even go into them at night because they'd cut ya! I remember one time, an old cowboy, named Newt, was drunk after a parade and rode his horse right inside the building while we were playing pool. I'm telling you, it was a crazy lifestyle.

We loved playing pool. In fact, my wife was really good and used to be able to run a table. A lot of people would call her a "sleeper" because she'd act like she couldn't play. She'd let you get a few balls in and then...POW! She'd just clean the house. She could run a table and put all those balls away in pretty short order.

Shortly after coming back into fellowship, we had some Christian friends across the street. They were a safe couple who were both saved and listened to Brother Hagin. They had a really nice home and a pool table. Of course, being neighbors and friends, they invited us to come over and play pool quite often.

Sally really enjoyed playing pool, and she wanted to go play with these neighbors. But I never would go and she didn't understand why. She would say, "Hon, come on. It's not at a bar. They're Christians. They don't drink or anything else and there'll probably be Christian music playing on the stereo. Let's just go play."

I had to tell her, "Honey, I can't because I'm too close to what I just came out of," meaning the alcoholic lifestyle, "and pool ties me to it." Please understand me here. Playing pool is not a sin. But thank God for the Holy Ghost, because with His help, I knew enough not to go around and flirt with something I had just come out of.

Now, all these years later, I can go into any bar and sit down and preach Jesus to them and it wouldn't bother me a bit. They could even offer me a cold one all iced up and it wouldn't tempt me a bit. I'd sit right there and all the ice would just melt right off of it and I'd never touch it. But there was a day when I knew, *"Don't go around that yet,"* because the Holy Ghost was teaching me how to govern my lower nature.

Going Back to the Vomit

Some of you reading this book have been flirting with some stuff. Don't flirt with it. You must get stronger. If you do, it will drag you back. The devil has been lying to some of you telling you, "Well, you need to go back in that to testify to them folks about the goodness of God." You don't need to go yet. You need more WORD. You need to renew your soul. Because, if you don't follow the Holy Ghost and renew your soul, when you go back, you'll stay.

*¹ Paul, an apostle of Jesus Christ by the will of God, to the **saints which are at***

120

> *Ephesus, and to the faithful in Christ Jesus:*
>
> *2 Grace be to you, and peace, from God our Father, and from The LORD Jesus Christ. (Ephesians 1:1-2, KJV, emphasis added)*

So, according to Ephesians 1:1-2, who is the book of Ephesians written to? To the Saints (or Christians) at Ephesus. Now, let's jump over to chapter 4.

> *22 That ye **put off concerning the former conversation of the old man**, which is corrupt according to the deceitful lusts; (Ephesians 4:22, KJV, emphasis added)*

Now, to keep this straight, let me ask this one more time. Who was this letter written to? To the Saints at Ephesus. In other words, to the church – to the saved folks. In verse 22, the phrase, *"...put off the former conversation of the old man,"* means to stop living by the lower nature or the flesh nature. Remember what we've been learning. If your soul is saved, then it will side in with the spirit man, and you can control your flesh.

You can tell when a Christian is really studying the WORD and renewing their mind. They are on fire for God, living victoriously, and nothing really disturbs them. But here's the thing. If that same Christian stops reading the WORD, quits praying in tongues, and starts coasting, eventually, stuff will start to bother them. You don't just stall out and stay at the same level when you quit. Soon enough, the people who quit seem like they are backing up[90] and headed toward the old lifestyle again.

---

90 Mark 4:24-25

Say out loud, "I ain't backing up!" No! We don't want to return to the vomit that we just threw up[91]. Trust me here, if you let your soul go crazy and you quit reading the WORD, then you'll go back. Maybe not today. Maybe not tomorrow. But, eventually, you will go back. I know this by the instruction of the WORD of God and the Holy Ghost. But I also know this from personal experience.

A bit after the invitation to play pool with the neighbors, Sally and I went to her brother's house in Hilton, Oklahoma. We all worked in the oil patch and we worked hard. At that time, my thoughts were along the lines of, "Well, you can drink. You won't hurt anything. You're saved."

So, on the way to Hilton that day, I stopped and bought a 12-pack of beer. I sat there at my brother-in-law's and drank it all, and I remember I couldn't even get drunk. The whole time I was drinking, down inside my spirit (not my mind), I kept hearing, "This ain't right. This ain't right. Stop this." That was my spirit scratching at my soul. But, you know what? You can override your spirit man if your soul is goofy. So that day was the last time I ever drank.

We had been going to an Assembly of God church in Davis. But, even then I could tell God had more available for us and I needed it! I told my wife, "There ain't enough power here to hold me steady. I need something that's going to bring life into me, because I'm too shaky right now." So, we found a church over in Sulfur. It was a good thing because I was about to be tested on it again.

A short time later, another couple we were friends with took us to Oklahoma City to some high dollar horse shows and stuff. I mean these were fancy high dollar sales. When you pulled up, the valets were wearing cowboy tuxes and they'd open doors for you and all kinds of stuff. They even had carpet on the arena floor where they brought the horses through, and if the horse pooped, they just swept it up. The problem with these events was that they expected you to drink. Everybody had a wine glass – everybody. They all called it social drinking, because they all had money, therefore nobody had a problem. But, by this time, I had learned. I had renewed my mind, and I wouldn't drink.

I'm sure a lot of people wondered about us that day because we just kept passing on the alcohol. But it's OK. I knew we were doing things God's way. It may not have made sense to everyone around us, but we had learned to follow the Holy Ghost and that was all that mattered. We also learned that you can still have a ball at events like this even without a drop of liquor in you.

God's Way Doesn't Make Sense to the World

God's way may not seem fun to the people around you and it probably won't even make sense to them. But if you'll faithfully follow Him, He'll make sure and take you on the best ride of your life. But you must have your mind renewed so you can listen carefully, act boldly, and stand firmly.

Not too long ago, the LORD told us to purchase a piece of property for a new church building. At the time, our banker told us, "Well, that's really high for this area, Ricky." But we had it in our heart, because the LORD told us to do it.

So we said, "Well, let's look at all the paperwork and see where you are."

"Are you really sure you want it?" he replied.

"Yeah, I want it. The LORD said to get it."

"Can we just get it cheaper?" he asked.

Eventually, the seller did come down $80,000. So, I went back to this man and said, "Are you guys going to go with us or not?"

He answered, "Well, you know, on paper we just can't make it work."

I said, "Well, I ain't talking to you about what's on paper. You know me. I'm not a nut. I'm not a flake. We pay our bills and take care of business. The LORD said buy it, now are y'all going to help me or not?" He finally agreed to help us. So we bought it and signed on it.

You know what happened? Just a year later, all the land in that particular area has now doubled and some of it has tripled because of all the oil wells drilling everywhere. Now, they're all like, "Boy! That was a good deal!" But in the beginning they couldn't see it. Sometimes, God's ways don't make sense to the world and they have trouble going with you on the things He tells you to do. But you can't let that stop you. Just keep on trucking and doing what the Holy Spirit told you to do.

Later, we were going to buy another piece of real estate. So my wife and I had to do a full fiscal report with profit and loss analysis and some other detailed reports on another business. So, the banker was looking at this and he called me and said, "Ricky, I really need to talk to you."

So, I went in and he said quite concerned, "Where did all this money go from your XYZ business?"

I answered truthfully, "It went to the church."

"I didn't see it as an expenditure or anything, so I couldn't figure out where this money went," he replied, "What are you doing with it?"

"Well, that's our tithe off that business."

"You can't do that!" he exclaimed, "That's too much money!"

"Yes I can, it's my business!" The thought of it just messed with him because he doesn't operate by the same system that we do. God's ways don't make sense to the world. The world says to get all you can, and step on anybody you need to in order to get to the top. But God says the opposite. He says in order to get ahead you need to sow through tithes and offerings. The Scripture also says to prefer your brother over yourself, do things ethically right, and be a person of integrity.

In general, the WORD rubs people the wrong way. My wife has often testified about the time when we were in Bible School. I don't know what our annual salary was back then, but it was very low. We had to pay tuition, rent, and everything else out of it. We were paying about $400-500 per month back then for just tuition and rent. That was most of our money! Now, this was in the mid-80s and what we made was not nearly enough to cover our expenses every month, but as we were faithful to tithe, God was faithful to provide. I honestly do not know how everything got paid.

When we share this testimony, people get upset and tell me, "Well, all they want is my money." Usually these folks mean pastors and evangelists, such as myself, when they say this. The truth is we could care less about your money. I'm serious. I've got a God that loves me and He takes real good care of me.

But sometimes, people want to prostitute their money and if their pastor won't do what they want him to do, they threaten to pull their tithes. Here's the deal with that. If they do quit tithing or leave their church, they aren't operating by Kingdom Principles or being led by the Spirit. It won't go well. Usually, their health, family, or finances end up affected sooner or later. Unsaved people in the world operate that way. They will use their power and influence to manipulate others to try to get them to do stuff they don't want to do.

A carnal mind will fight a Christian about tithing, because it doesn't make sense. But your spirit knows it works and a renewed mind knows it works. You can still get to the top, and when you get there, you get to stay there if you go by the way of the WORD and do it God's way.

> ⁶ Now **the mind of the flesh [which is sense and reason without the Holy Spirit] is death** [death that comprises all the miseries arising from sin, both here and hereafter]. But the mind of the [Holy] Spirit is life and [soul] peace [both now and forever].
>
> ⁷ [That is] because **the mind of the flesh [with its carnal thoughts and purposes] is hostile to God,** for **it does not submit itself to God's Law;** indeed it cannot. (Romans 8:6-7, AMP, emphasis added)

Now, look at verse seven. It says, "...*the mind of the flesh [with its carnal thoughts and purposes] is hostile to God, for it does not submit itself to God's Law...*" Let me ask you, what is the

Law that governs the Church? The Law of Love[92]. The carnal mind, or the soul, is hostile to God because it cannot operate by the Law of Love. This is why we must learn to lead with our spirit, because we ought to be motivated by love in everything we do.

Not Everyone in a Limo is What You Think

The carnal, unrenewed mind, makes judgments about people. It is the part that is vulnerable to the fiery darts and slippery suggestions of the devil. For example, the devil wants Christians to be broke, but God doesn't. So then, why would the church ever fight being rich? Because they've not heeded Romans 12:1-2 and they're under the influence of the world. Here's the deal, if Christians have all the money we need, then we're going to send our kids to Christian schools and Bible schools, we're going to finance all the missionaries, we're going to build all the buildings, and we're going to do *everything* God has planned. But the devil is going to fight that in a number of ways. For example, assumption is a subtle dart of the devil that few Christians recognize. Unfortunately, once it hits a target, it easily opens the door to demonic weapons such as judgment and offense.

A few years back, we were in Bakersfield, California. A couple of guys were traveling with me on that trip. The pastor had reserved a really nice place for us to stay. He had come up to visit with us for a little bit before the evening service. Well, when we all came down that evening to head to the church, there was a great big white limousine stretched out there and the driver was wearing a tux – complete with hat and gloves. As we came out the door, he said, "Mr. Edwards?"

---

92 Luke 10:27-28 and Galatians 5:6

"Yes?" I answered.

"I'm here to pick you up and take you to church."

And I'm like, "Sweet!" We drove around for about an hour to get to the church. There were non-alcoholic refreshments and everything else we needed back there. We could roll the window down and talk to the driver if we needed something. I mean, this was top-notch!

But do you know what happened when we pulled up to that church? All the people had this puzzled look on their face like, "Who is that?" They all assumed it was a pimp daddy or a rock star pulling up. That thinking is under the influence of the world. See if you're a minister or a righteous man, and if you show up like that, the first thought that comes to a lot of people's minds is, "He's got to be scamming, because there's no way he can get that just through the law of giving his tithes and offerings."

That's a lie of the devil. I watch flights, car rentals and things like that. I'm frugal, but I learned a long time ago that I don't have to be stingy. I will admit, it took several years to get my thinking squared out and you know I'm not completely all the way there yet. But I know I'm headed somewhere, and if it takes me the rest of my life, I'm going to get there.

Offense Opens the Door to Sickness

Years ago God called an American man to go to Russia to start a church. He and his wife were obedient to do that. In fact, they still have a large ministry over there still today.

At about the same time, my wife and I were friends with another couple here in the States. We went around and ministered with them quite a bit. Eventually, they were called to go over to Russia and to help with the ministry being established there. Our friends went and were there for about a year.

It's important to remember that when we work for someone or for an organization, we don't always understand the number of the decisions that have to be made or understand why they are decided one way over another. We must make absolutely sure that we do not make any assumptions about what is going on or why. During the process of time, some things had transpired with the ministry, and the pastors of the church in Russia had to make some decisions that my friends didn't understand. Because of this, they became hurt, left Russia, and got out of the ministry altogether.

Recently, my friend texted me from the ICU. He had been dealing with cancer for the last six months and he didn't have much hope to survive it. Remember, this is someone I used to preach with. I'm teaching you about the soul because that's how the cancer got into this man. He was hurt emotionally and that opened the door for the devil to get in. This is why we must keep our minds renewed to the WORD of God – so things like this don't have a way in.

Grudges Open Doors and Bring Storms So Build in Times of Peace

In the Scriptures, the word "elder" doesn't mean old like we think of today. It means to be mature in the things of the Spirit. So, in the Body of Christ, you can be 50 years old and still be just as carnal as everyone else in the world – hold grudges, give people the silent treatment, etc.

For my friend, the cancer has already established a stronghold. He's already lost over 100 pounds. We can always pray. Prayer is powerful. But, at this point in time, when there's such a stronghold, I don't know exactly what to pray.

So, I asked him, "What about that thing you were holding onto?"

He said, "When I got sick, I released it."

Well, that's good. But the time to release it is before you get into any trouble. Because if you don't, you'll have to deal with the issue *AND* the sickness, or the debt, or whatever else it is the devil brings through that open door. If you've already been struggling in your soul (or emotions) to the point that you can even allow yourself to hold a grudge, then you'll have to work on your soul, and deal with the sickness, and deal with the pain, and so on. Do you see, this thing can get real out of hand and get real rough real quick?

That's why Psalm 127:1 says, *"Except the LORD build the house, they labour in vain that build it..." (KJV)*. When I was at Rhema, Brother Hagin used to say, *"Don't build a house in the time of the storm, build it when you are at peace."* In other words, build your faith by going to church, studying the WORD deeply, praying in tongues daily, and building your relationship with Christ when life is easy — in times of peace. Because, once the storms of life come blowing, you can build but it is much more difficult. Let me show you what I mean with a natural example.

When you are working on a roof, you can get a 4'x8' sheet of plywood in a 10 mile per hour wind and it will whip you all over everywhere! But then, when there is no wind, you can pick it up and walk all over that roof with no trouble. Along the same lines, if you have a flagpole and the flag is standing straight out, you know it is not the time to be tinning a roof with 40' sheets of tin. You can do it, but someone is likely to cut, to get hurt, or even blown off the roof.

So, Christians who refuse to do anything with their soul will have to build in the time of the storm whenever trouble arrives. Don't wait until sickness is in your body to build or study the WORD on healing. Build your faith on healing when you are healthy and your body is at peace. Say out loud, "I'm glad I don't hold grudges! I'm glad I'm not an emotional wreck!"

Everyone has had someone hurt them, whether it was intentional or not, it doesn't matter. We've all gotten mad over something. Here's some practical wisdom to help you release that grudge and stay steady in your emotions: Pray right now to forgive them. Forgiving someone doesn't mean that you agree with what they did. It also doesn't mean that you will somehow magically forget what happened. It means you refuse to allow the devil to hold *you* hostage over that situation any longer.

After you've prayed to forgive them, if you still feel that anger want to rise up when you see them again, just don't go around them for a while. You need more time. The worst thing you can do is get around them and then go off somewhere and start talking bad about them. When you do that, you feed that resentment. That ends up hurting you not them[93]. So, just stay away for a time and continue to renew your mind with the WORD. Soon enough, you'll find your soul has lined up with your spirit man and you have moved past the emotions. At that point, you've truly released it.

---

[93] Proverbs 6:2

Chapter 12 – Victory Over Carnality Means Taking Action

Carnality in Christians is not a new or isolated concept. We've already seen that James wrote to the Church at Jerusalem and told them they were carnal. Well, Paul said something similar when he wrote to the Church of Corinth. Let's look at it very carefully in both the King James and the New Living Translations both.

> [7] *So that **ye come behind in no gift;** waiting for the coming of our Lord Jesus Christ: (1 Corinthians 1:7, KJV, emphasis added)*

> [7] *Now **you have every spiritual gift you need** as you eagerly wait for the return of our Lord Jesus Christ. (1Corinthians 1:7, NLT, emphasis added)*

When we look at these two translations of the 1 Corinthians 1:7, we can see that the Church at Corinth did not lack in any of the spiritual gifts (i.e., word of wisdom, word of knowledge, faith, healings, miracles, prophecy, discerning of spirits, speaking in tongues, and interpretation of tongues[94]). Let's see what else he had to say about them:

> [18] *I thank my God, I speak with tongues **more than ye all**: (1 Corinthians 14:18, KJV, emphasis added)*

---

[94] Romans 12:1-11

If Paul spoke in tongues more than them, then we know they must have spoken in tongues as well. We also know they did not come behind or lack in any gifts. So, from these two verses, we can tell that the Christians at Corinth were born-again, spirit-filled, had all the gifts, and allowed those gifts to operate among them. But look at the surprising statement Paul makes to them:

> *3And I, brethren, could not speak unto you as unto **spiritual**, but as unto **carnal**, even as unto **babes in Christ**. (1 Corinthians 3:1, KJV, emphasis added)*

> *3 Dear brothers and sisters, when I was with you I couldn't talk to you as I would to **spiritual people**. I had to talk as though you **belonged to this world** or as though you were **infants in Christ**. (1 Corinthians 3:1, NLT, emphasis added)*

These men and women were saved. They were Christians, but just like the Christians James wrote to, their souls were not yet saved. Here again, we see that even though someone is saved, born-again, and spirit-filled, if the soul is not renewed and developed by the WORD, then the soul and the flesh will side in together. This alliance allows the devil to dominate the Christian and harass them through that open doorway – even though they are born-again and children of God. One could say these Corinthians were still in spiritual diapers and trying to drink from a spiritual bottle so to speak. They hadn't matured beyond that first stage of spiritual development. That's why he called them infants in Christ.

Now, let's jump over to Galatians:

> *1Now I say, That the heir, as long as he is a child, differeth nothing from a servant, though he be lord of all; (Galatians 4:1, KJV)*

We see this in the natural too. As long as the heir is a child, even if his father is already gone, he doesn't enjoy any of the things his father left for him. Why not? Because he is under age and is not mature yet. That's what Galatians 4:1 is telling us from a spiritual perspective. We have to grow up and mature in the things of Christ in order to benefit from everything our Father intends for us to have. Additionally, underage and immature children are the most vulnerable to bullies. That's why Satan likes to keep people from studying the WORD and growing up. Say out loud, "I'm growing up!"

Toker – Dope Smoker

We used to have a church member who smoked, and I'm not talking about cigarettes. He was a toker. In other words, he had a pair of hemostats and he wasn't a nurse. He used to tell me, "You know, God made marijuana. Besides, it's legal in a lot of states." He would go on and on with his rationalizations. Basically, he was trying to get me to tell him it was ok.

But, I had to tell him, "Brother, I used to smoke dope. I didn't just smoke dope either. My friends and I would find mushrooms that wouldn't completely kill you and make tea out of them to take trips without ever leaving the farm! I mean all that. I've been there! But then I got saved and I learned there was a better way to live my life."

Remember, earlier in this book, I told you about going to Hilton, OK and trying to get drunk after I was saved. Something on the inside of me kept telling me it was wrong and to quit it. That wasn't my wife. She never jumped on me or said a word to me. Every beer I opened up that day tasted so terrible! It hurt me on the inside because I knew it wasn't right. It was the Holy Spirit inside me talking to me. The deal of it is, if you'll just pay attention to where the life and the nature of God was imparted into you, then you'll be OK. He'll guide you out of whatever has you trapped.

I've heard it said that the definition of insanity is doing the same thing over and over again expecting a different result. Remember, anybody who lives out of the soul that isn't saved will always continue to do what they used to do. Things won't really change. But, if you learn to live from where the life and nature of God was imparted – in your born again spirit – then you'll see things begin to turn around.

Many times, however, these habits and ways of life become so ingrained in a person, that they become an open doorway for the devil to bring shame, guilt, and condemnation. That's why we have to renew our mind with the WORD and truly understand the relationships between the spirit, soul, flesh, sin, and the Divine Nature imparted into us at salvation. We cannot afford to be confused on these issues if we are to live victoriously in all areas of life here on Planet Earth.

I Don't Need Holiness – I Have Liberty

A lot of people will try to justify the things they do with their bodies by pointing to liberty and grace. I've said it before, and the Bible makes it very clear, if you don't have a body, you aren't here. Your body doesn't get saved when you do. So, let's take a quick look at what we are supposed to do with our bodies:

> I beseech you therefore, brethren, by the mercies of God, that ye **present your bodies a living sacrifice, holy, acceptable unto God**, which is your

reasonable service. (Romans 12:1, KJV,
emphasis added)

Christians are supposed to present our bodies as living sacrifices, *"holy and acceptable unto God."* This contradicts a whole lot of stuff they're teaching out there in the Body of Christ these days. I can hear someone now, "Wait a minute, if you're saved, you can do anything you want. You're covered by the Blood."

If that's true, then we're just going to have to rip Romans 12:1 right out of the Bible! Men shacking up with other women while they're still married to someone else, drinking, carousing, and carrying on like the world when they're supposed to be saved – how is that presenting your body as a living sacrifice, holy and acceptable to God?

I'm not saying these people aren't saved. But I will tell you this, if you push that too far, then you'll live a completely defeated life and possibly lose everything. See, you might want to do something with your body and if your soul isn't saved it will go right along. That means you will live a carnal Christian's life. You'll be held hostage and yoked to something that has your spirit man screaming, "I really don't want to live this way!" Eventually, the natural consequences of those choices (e.g., sickness, poverty, jails, institutions, or even death) will catch up to you.

I believe in holiness. But holiness isn't what most people think. It isn't about the way you dress. It simply means separated for God. When someone's mind gets renewed to the WORD of God on holiness, the Holy Ghost will take care of everything else on the outside.

Some of the things people say such as, "Well, you know, I'm saved and I have liberty according to Galatians 5:13. I have the liberty to do this or that, and I don't think God will hold it against me."

We do have liberty. But they are only looking at the first part of that verse:

> *For, brethren, ye have been called unto liberty; only* ***use not liberty for an occasion to the flesh****, but by love serve one another. (Galatians 5:13, KJV, emphasis added)*

It goes on to say don't use your liberty to indulge your flesh. People don't like to hear about holiness. In fact, it usually brings a great calm over the church that rivals the one after the storm Jesus rebuked[95]. Like I said, I believe in holiness. But it's not an outward show in long dresses, and no make-up, and hair standing up like a bee hive. Holiness is of an inward work that will show up on the outside.

Be a Doer Not a Hearer Only

In Luke 11:15-26, Jesus was teaching about how to deal with the devil. More specifically, He was teaching that a strong man can keep his goods in peace until a stronger man comes along and overtakes him[96]. Additionally, He explained that when an evil spirit is kicked out of its house it goes around looking for another house and if it can't find one it goes back to the first one. If nothing has taken its place, then it moves back in and brings seven

---

[95] Mark 4:39

[96] Luke 11:21-22

of its buddies with it – making the person worse than at first[97]. But then look what happens when He gets to verse 27:

> *27 And it came to pass, as he spake these things, a certain woman of the company lifted up her voice, and said unto him, Blessed is the womb that bare thee, and the paps which thou hast sucked. (Luke 11:27, KJV)*

In other words, this woman basically jumped up and exclaimed in excitement, "Who's your momma?" right in the middle of His sermon. He's teaching about how to deal with the devil, how to be effective and victorious, and how the devil gets a foothold in people's lives and this woman jumps up and shouts, "Who's your momma?" Look carefully at Jesus' response:

> *28 But he said, Yea rather, blessed are they that hear the word of God, and keep it. (Luke 11:28, KJV)*

He said the truly blessed are the ones that hear the WORD and *do* it. In the middle of His sermon she wants to know who His family is, but He says it really doesn't matter who they are. That's not the main thing. The main thing is the WORD. The emphasis is the WORD. We cannot just hear the WORD, but when we hear it, we must also practice it.

James reminds us of this and explains why it is so important that we be doers of the WORD:

> *22 But be ye doers of the word, and not hearers only, deceiving your own selves. (James 1:22, KJV)*

When we are hearers only, there is no difference between us and the world. We become weak and easy targets for the devil to

---

[97] Luke 11:24-26

beat up on. The only way to stay strong and victorious in life is to keep our mind renewed to the WORD of God and to constantly be practicing what it says. When we do that, we will know who we are, and what is ours as children of the Most High God. We will also start to look and act differently from the rest of the world.

Unfortunately, we run into Christians acting like the world all the time and they'll try to make us out to be an oddball because we won't join them. It isn't always easy or comfortable being mature and keeping your flesh under control. Let me share a couple examples of what I'm talking about. I'm sure you'll recognize similar situations that may have popped up in your own life:

Once at a Chamber of Commerce meeting, a guy who taught Sunday School at another church here in Pawnee mentioned, "Well, we would offer long neck Buds at our function, but Pastor Ricky is here."

I said, "No, that's fine. You go ahead and drink if you want to. It don't bother me a bit."

He justified, "Well, you know, I can drink and be saved."

I replied, "That's fine. I used to drink and then I got saved. But you do what you want. If you want to drink, go ahead. But, I know what drinking did for me. I ended up in jail all the time. I was broke all the time, and I had whiskey dents on every corner of my vehicle. So, I know what that life leads to. If you want to do that, I believe you're saved. But I'm endeavoring to live a life different from everybody else." He wanted to make me feel like an outsider or a square peg because I didn't drink, but I wasn't going to wear that hat.

Consider also, I don't listen to off-color jokes and I don't laugh at them either. That can make for some uncomfortable moments. Over time, I've come to accept the fact that some people will think I'm an oddball because of it — but God doesn't.

I'm sure you can relate. But here's the thing, we aren't the oddballs! We're the ones making a stand for something to the best of our ability. We're not better. We simply want to live healthy, victorious, and blessed lives!

I don't want the people out there who aren't saved to think there is no difference between them and those who are saved. There is a separation from the Christian and the people who aren't saved. It ought to be clear to everyone.

Renew Your Soul for the Power to Flow

A few years back, we had a powerful move of the Spirit in Amarillo, Texas. I mean, the power of The LORD was so thick I could hardly walk. In that meeting, there was a lady who was having all kinds of problems. The LORD told me to go minister to her. So I headed that way, but before I could even get to her, she was healed, delivered, and completely set free. It was so wonderful.

That night, The LORD spoke to my heart and said, "Isn't it amazing how many people long for my power on them to help humanity. Yet they refuse to live separated lives so that my power might be able to abide."

Think back to John 5:26 for a moment. It says, *"For as the Father has life…" (KJV)*. This is the Zoë life as God has it. Then it goes on to say, *"…so hath he given to the Son to have life in himself" (KJV)*. Think of it this way, God took the life of God which He had, and put it into His Son, Jesus. Then Jesus said, "I've come and whoever'll accept me, I'm going to put that same life of God on the inside of them."

John G. Lake[98] got a revelation of this as he meditated on 1 John 4:4. He started to realize, "I've literally got the life of God on the inside of me. Not probably or figuratively, I literally have the life of God in me." He started boldly praying, "Dear Lord, when I lay hands on people, since I've got Your life flowing through me, they will be healed."

Consequently, it's recorded that one night he put his hand on a man with some type of belly trouble in a healing line. Such power of God went out of him, that it is reported that when he took his hand off, and the man opened his shirt, there was a black hand print on his belly. Now, this man was white. It didn't burn the man's skin, but there was so much power that it left a black imprint like he got hold of something electrical. That wasn't human power that was The Anointing.

So, naturally, people were surprised and asked him what did that. Lake's response was, "I got a revelation that greater is He that's *in* me," he said, "But I had to get my soul renewed so I could keep my body in control so this type of power could flow through me." You've got the same Anointing within and upon as well. All born-again Christians have the life of God in us. But you've got to

---

98 John G. Lake (1870-1935) was an anointed minister who saw many hundreds of thousands of divine healings during the course of his work for The Lord. You can read more about his life and ministry in his book *"John G. Lake –The Apostle of Divine Healing- The Life and Ministry of John G. Lake."* (Who was John G. Lake?)

get your soul renewed to understand how to operate with it properly.

Think on this for a minute. People jump and shout in services every week, "Send the power LORD! Send the power!" Yet, have you really thought about it? If you had the full power of God and your soul isn't saved what would that be like? Because if you think like the world, act like the world, and talk like the world, you might really do some damage to somebody. You might short circuit something. Have you ever thought about what it would be like if every single word you said came to pass immediately – not just the happy prospering ones – but the negative ones too? What about the words you snap at your spouse or your kids when they get under skin or when someone cuts you off in traffic on the way to work in the morning? God has to be able to trust you with the power He gives you because the gifts and calls of God are without repentance[99].

Renew Your Mind to Stay Free from the Devil's Traps

In John 10:10, Jesus said the thief comes to steal, to kill, and to destroy, but He came to give us life in all its abundance. Thank God for the abundant life. If you'll get your soul renewed to this kind of thinking, you'll laugh when a pain or something comes because you know the Greater One lives on the inside of you. In other words, the deck is stacked in your favor.

The other day I had to make a quick run out to Lake Havasu and the surrounding area. I made about 4,000 miles in four days. I was driving, listening to CDs, and having a ball. Then

---

[99] Romans 11:29

suddenly, there was such a pain that came in this left wrist that I couldn't even pick up a cup of coffee.

Now, that's serious to me because I am a coffee connoisseur! I know all about coffee. I have studied coffee. Yet, here I was, I couldn't even hold a cup of coffee and I started laughing. I thought, "That's so funny Devil."

And he's like, "Oh, you feel that? That's some of that carpal tunnel. That could be arthritis from all the work over the years."

See he's talking to me, but I've already taken time to renew my mind. So I immediately answer him, "Oh no, the Bible says I've got the life of God in me! Glory to God! And by the stripes of Jesus I'm healed!"

Now that wrist hurt badly for about four hours. I mean it hurt. It was throbbing and stuff, but I kept after it. Finally, I felt that power start rising up out of there and that pain went out of my hand and never came back. It's not ever coming back either. Every born again believer has that life on the inside of them, and it's life the way God lives it.

If you've given your life to Christ, then it's on the inside of you too. So when a disease or pain comes against you, start thinking about how much greater is He that is living right there inside you than that sickness or the pain that is trying to come on you and that thing will dissolve and fall off. But, remember, if your mind hasn't been renewed, it will fight you and when the devil says, "You feel that? Oh you got it." Your mind will reply, "Oh God, I hope not," and then he's snared you by your own words[100].

---

100 Proverbs 6:2

Chapter 13 – Make God's Thoughts Your Thoughts

To renew your mind is to give your mind a new way of thinking. When you renew your mind with the WORD of God, you're taking God's thoughts and making them your own. You are replacing your old way of thinking with how God thinks. A dear friend of mine, Pastor Nancy Dufresne puts it this way, "To renew your mind is to give your mind a new definition – God's definition." The carnal mind, will reason, argue, and struggle against the WORD. The Bible is our answer. So, if I'm arguing against the WORD, then I'm arguing against my answer. Most people don't even realize they are arguing with their answer.

Now, most of us would agree that just because someone isn't a tither doesn't mean his favorite cat or dog is going to die. And, just because someone doesn't believe in divine healing, most of the time, it doesn't mean that person will die from a regular sickness, like an infection or a cold. However, oftentimes people will say things like, "Now, I know God heals. But..." Then they will explain and justify why they have symptoms in their body. That's arguing with the WORD which says, *"...by whose stripes ye were healed" (1 Peter 2:24, KJV)*. Their faith is 80% yesterday and 20% today – up and down like a roller coaster. It is based on their natural senses rather than what the WORD says.

Don't ever feel bad if you have symptoms in your body. Always remember Romans 8:1. Highlight it in your Bible and memorize it. Use it to quench those fiery darts every time you start to feel bad about some part of your faith walk that isn't where you think it should be yet.

> *There is therefore **now no condemnation** to them which are in Christ Jesus, who walk not after the flesh, but after the Spirit. (Romans 8:1, KJV, emphasis added)*

Don't ever be condemned if you have sickness attack your body. Don't be condemned if you aren't in the place of prosperity that you want to be in yet. Do not live in condemnation. Nobody I know of has arrived and does this perfectly — not anyone. We are all pressing to go after something. But, thank God, there is no condemnation for us because we are all at different places.

Keep a Firm Grip

Faith is of the heart. According to Romans 10:10, we believe with the heart. That means you believe God with your spirit not your mind.

> *[10] For with the heart man believeth unto righteousness; and with the mouth confession is made unto salvation. (Romans 10:10, KJV)*

By renewing the mind, your soul will quickly agree with the WORD it hears and the faith in your spirit. It won't fight, oppose, argue, or struggle with it; rather, it will agree. Brother Hagin made this statement, "A spiritual giant is someone whose heart and mind agree." The renewing of the mind is a process and it takes an investment of time. Remember, your mind doesn't stay renewed any more than your hair stays combed. You cannot skip several days of renewing your mind without consequences.

> *Therefore we ought to give the more*
> *earnest heed to the things which we*
> *have heard, lest at any time we should*
> ***let them slip****. (Hebrews 2:1, KJV, emphasis*
> *added)*

According to the Interlinear Bible, the original Greek meaning of the phrase, *"let them slip"* was, *"to run out as leaking vessels."* The Message translation says, *"...keep a firm grip on what we've heard so that we don't drift off."* Of course, it means that we don't drift off from the truth. So, the continual renewing of the mind is a process. We must do it every day so we don't lose what we have learned, and to ensure we stay on the correct course.

Back in the late 80s and early 90s, my wife and I would minister between seven and ten times per week – every week. We did that for almost ten years. We were busy starting churches, doing live radio, and other things along those lines. I had very little time to study. Mostly, I studied very late at night from 11:30 p.m. to 3 or 4 o'clock in the morning. I was very studious and did this almost every night.

But you know what I've noticed? If I don't continually go back over those Scriptures, I'll forget things and my mind will get clouded. Then I'll get to thinking stuff that isn't right. With all of that study...I still have to study. It's just like my hair. I combed it this morning, but if I don't touch it again, by the time you see me tomorrow afternoon you'll be suggesting that I comb it again.

The thing is, right now, my hair looks great. It's all combed nice and neat. I bet yours is too. That's the tricky part about not reading your Bible and praying in tongues every day. At first, you're too busy one day so you skip and there doesn't seem to be any consequences. But, soon enough, you'll be able to tell, because your mind will be out of whack – even though you are saved. That's why busyness is a favorite tool of the enemy.

146

THE SOUL

Conversations and Attitudes

Remember in Ephesians 4:22 of the King James Version, *"That you put off the former conversations..."* The word "conversations" means manner of life, lifestyle, or the way you live. Let's look at verses 22-23 again in the Amplified version:

> ²² Strip yourselves of your former nature [put off and discard your old unrenewed self] which characterized your previous **manner of life** and becomes corrupt through lusts and desires that spring from delusion;
>
> ²³ And **be constantly renewed in the spirit of your mind** [having a fresh mental and spiritual attitude] (Ephesians 4:22-23, AMP, emphasis added)

In both the King James and the Amplified translations, when Paul writes, "...be constantly renewed in the spirit of your mind...," we need to look carefully and make sure we truly understand what he's saying. Now, we know that he cannot be talking about our spirit man because that was made brand new at salvation. The Amplified makes it a little easier for us to see this phrase is dealing with the soul because it further clarifies in verse 23 that we are to have, *"...a fresh mental and spiritual attitude."*

Let's take healing as an example of how this works. An "old" conversation or attitude about healing would be that you can't be sure if it is God's will to heal someone because He might be trying to teach them a lesson through that sickness. There are also those who believe God can heal, but they will fight you for the right to believe that if somebody died it was still God's will. God isn't a twin. He's the only one. Let's think this through completely. You just told me that you believe healing belongs to a Christian, so if a Christian dies sick that cannot be God's will. If that last statement rubs you the wrong way, then your thinking is off.

Healing always belongs to Christians:

> *² Beloved, I wish above all things that thou mayest prosper and be in health, even as thy soul prospereth. (3 John 2, KJV)*

As you meditate on that Scripture and repeat it, you renew your mind by making God's thought your own thereby changing your attitude and conversation. You start to live differently. Things start to change. Health comes.

Brother Hagin often shared that his last headache was in August 1932. He would then say, "It's too late to start having headaches now!" Some Christians would get mad when he'd say that. He wasn't trying to upset anyone. He was just trying to show them, what can happen if you get your mind renewed to what's available to you. God wants you to walk in divine health.

Thank God for healing when you've been sick, but it's a whole lot better to *not* get upset with somebody and to *not* have sickness attack you in the first place. Then you don't have to believe God to heal you. When you think about it, it's just a whole lot better to walk in love and walk in health. Because once sickness gets a hold of you, then you have to get it off of you.

Sometimes people sit around waiting for God to do something for them. But, the blessings of God don't just fall on us like ripe cherries falling off a tree. We have to do something – renew our minds and use our faith. Think of 3 John 2 this way, to the degree that your soul (not your spirit) is prospering in an area, or increasing in knowledge of the WORD and faith, so will you increase in that area of your life. That's why I could be as healthy as a horse and so broke I couldn't get out of town at the same time. I had renewed my mind in one area so my soul was prospering in that area, but I had neglected the other.

Check the Beam in Your Eye

I remember, one time, God asked me by the Holy Ghost, "Can the blind lead the blind?"

"Why no," I replied.

He responded, "Then how did they both fall into the ditch if they can't?" and then He asked me, "Can two walk together except they agree[101]?"

I answered, "No."

"Yes, they can. But they're always fighting and pulling and scratching," He said.

> *39 And he spake a parable unto them, Can the blind lead the blind? shall they not both fall into the ditch?*
>
> *40 The disciple is not above his master: but every one that is perfect shall be as his master.*
>
> *41 And why beholdest thou the mote that is in thy brother's eye, but perceivest not the beam that is in thine own eye?*
>
> *42 Either how canst thou say to thy brother, Brother, let me pull out the mote that is in thine eye, when thou thyself beholdest not the beam that is in thine own eye? Thou hypocrite, cast out first the beam out of thine own eye, and then shalt thou see clearly to pull out the*

---

101 Amos 3:3

149

mote that is in thy brother's eye. (Luke 6:39-42, KJV)

In Luke 6:39-40 Jesus is talking about leadership and who you submit to. In verse 41, the word "mote" is a 2"x12" beam. So, in today's language it would be something like, "Why look at the speck in your brother's eye and ignore the 2"x12" hanging out of your own head?"

That beam He's talking about is like a bridge beam. Underneath a bridge, they don't use the old I-beam metal like they used to. These days they use big old concrete beams with a lot of rebar in them. Those concrete and rebar beams support the weight of the bridge.

In the parable, the beam Jesus is talking about is something that supports the way you see things in life. The beam is the part of your thinking that controls the way you see things. That's why Jesus says it is in your eye – it is a filter. This is the reason most people bump into each other and don't see eye to eye on a particular issue. They are two different people with two different ways of seeing the world. Jesus says, "Why beholdest the way somebody else sees something but you don't deal with how you see something?" The beam is a representation of what supports our beliefs.

For example, a person once tried hard to convince me that God *needed* a young man to die because several people gave their lives to Christ at his funeral. To this I said, "No. I cannot agree with that because the WORD doesn't support it. There was only one man qualified to die so that people would be saved. His name was Jesus." They had a beam in their thinking to support, or explain, why this man died young. The beam in our eye is what causes people to bump into each other – the way we perceive things. Ask yourself this question, "What supports the way you see things?"

Do You Really Understand God's Prosperity?

It is natural when we see a word, to immediately think of the most prevalent definition. Therefore, when most people see the WORD "prosperity" they probably think money or wealth. Well, to me, the word "prosperity" means to increase. In fact, according to Dictionary.com, it means a successful, flourishing, or thriving condition, and good fortune especially in financial respects. Notice it said *especially* in financial respects but not *only* in financial respects.

I tell this story everywhere I go. In Oklahoma as you get into the fall, it might be 80° one day and 40° the next until it finally decides to be winter. I remember years ago, one of our ushers, Brother Donny, testified to the fact that every year he would end up in the hospital with bronchitis and pneumonia. Sometimes, he'd end up back in the hospital two or three times a year. He said each time he would just listen to Scripture. He also said he wasn't ashamed because he'd call and say, "Hey Pastor, I'm in the hospital. Can you come pray for me?"

Did you catch that, he wasn't ashamed that he was sick. In fact, we were all grateful there was a hospital for him to go to get oxygen and medication to help him breathe and to help his body fight the infection. He knew his measure of faith and wasn't ashamed of it.

We'd go pray for him. He'd get healed and raised up. He was never ashamed that he had bronchitis, but he just kept listening to the WORD and studying – renewing his mind. Do you know what? He hasn't been back in the hospital for that again. That's a thriving condition of health. That's increase. That's prosperity!

You have to understand, this didn't happen for him overnight. It took a long time for him to get to the place where he no longer got bronchitis in the winter. He had to recognize where the old rotten beams were in his thinking, and he had to keep renewing his mind with the WORD so those beams could be replaced. He had to get God's thoughts on healing and divine health down inside him and make them his own. He had to stay out of condemnation. He had to stay in faith.

He also had to learn to deal with his mind screaming, "You're sick, you're sick, you're sick!" and how to overrule the body which complained, "Can you not feel that?" But then, as his mind was continually renewed with the WORD and his soul was saved, then it joined in with spirit man which was already in agreement with God's Word. Since 2/3 majority wins, the body had no choice but to fall in line and the symptoms left. From that day forward, Brother Donny, never got bronchitis again. He's healed and whole. That's increase and fullness of health! That's prosperity!

Don't let the devil make you feel bad if you've ever been sick. Just realize we're seeking a place where we are never sick again. I can't go out and pay $100,000 cash for a house yet, but a day will come that I can if I'll keep believing. In the meantime, I don't beat myself up that I can't do it right now. I remember a time when I couldn't even buy a new tire. I had to go down to some place that sold used ones and believe God it would last long enough to get another used one. That's why the Bible says don't despise the days of small beginnings[102]. If you stay with it, small beginnings won't stay small. It takes a lifetime. So don't get upset that you're not where you want to be yet, just stay with it.

Wrong Thinking Leads to All Kinds of Mischief

So, why does the devil fight us so in the soulish realm? Because wrong thinking leads to wrong believing, and wrong believing leads to wrong speaking. Wrong speaking always opens the door for wrong things to happen. This concept is so important you should highlight it and write it down.

To illustrate this point, let me share a story that Brother Hagin shared often from his own life:

At one point in ministry, Brother Hagin had to sell his old car for junk to a salvage yard. Then he took off on foot or rode the Greyhound bus to his ministry commitments. He went to The LORD about Isaiah 1:19, which says, *"If ye be willing and obedient ye shall eat the good of the land"* (KJV).

He told God, "I'm not eating the good of the land. I'm three months behind on my rent. My kids aren't adequately clothed. Where am I missing it?"

God answered him, "Well, you have been obedient, but you haven't been willing." His heart had been disgruntled. So he quickly repented, changed his attitude, and things began to turn around.

---

102 Zechariah 4:10

Finally, he got to a point in his ministry where he thought he could get a brand new car. So, he checked with God and asked, "LORD would it be alright for me to buy this brand new car?"

The LORD answered him, "Yes, it'll be good. You've looked at the account books. You know what you can afford."

So, then he started bugging God about what kind of car to buy. Finally, The LORD told him, "I'm not going to ride in it you are. Get what you like." Eventually, he bought a brand new blue Cadillac.

A few months after purchasing it, things got really tight financially and he was upside down on the car. So, he made this statement, "I'm taking it back to the dealership and I know I'm going to lose money on it. But, it's just too hard."

Soon thereafter, Jesus appeared to him and told him, "If you take the car back, you will change your doctrine because wrong thinking always leads to wrong teaching. Your voice is too great in the Body of Christ for your teaching to be off[103]." Brother Hagin decided to believe Jesus and kept the car. I called their ministry office just the other day. You know what? They still have that blue Cadillac all these years later – even after he's gone on to be with the LORD!

Listen carefully, if someone's thinking is wrong, their teaching will be wrong. They have the wrong beams supporting their thinking. That's why people will fight and argue over doctrines that have no basis in Scripture. It is also why people believe God sends sickness to teach people a lesson, and why people all over the world believe God wants Christians to be poor.

---

[103] Ministers and Teachers, please look at Appendix 3 for a special word just for you on this subject.

But we know from Scripture that God doesn't use sickness or poverty to teach people, He uses the Holy Ghost.

Many times people are born again and on their way to Heaven, but they get stuck in the arena of sickness, poverty, or something else because they don't know or understand exactly what God has said in His Word. Most likely their doctrine is based on someone's experience rather than Scripture, and this caused their thinking to be confused, then the confused thinking led to a confused doctrine. I've seen it over and over, whenever people teach from *their experience* instead of the Bible, they will get off into a ditch on one side or the other. They say things like, "Well, you know Grandma, she loved God, but she died anyway."

When I hear comments like that, I reply, "I don't know what was in Grandma's heart. I'm not saying she didn't love God, but I can't go off of Grandma's, or Grandpa's, or Uncle Bubba's, or anyone else's experience. I've got to stay with what the WORD says." This is why it is so important to always check what the WORD says.

Along these same lines, I'll never forget a conversation I had a while back with a young man on this very topic. He and I were working on a church roof and he asked me a question. I immediately answered him with a Scripture and he said, "Okay. That answers that." Then he asked me another question.

I said, "You know, I don't know about that. But, I could give you my opinion."

He said, "I really don't care about your opinion. I'd rather know what the Bible says."

Do you know what I did? I shook that young man's hand and said, "I've done a pretty good job of teaching you."

Every doctrine should be backed up with Scripture. It should never be based solely on someone's experience or what they think; because, as we have seen, a person's thinking can get clouded and confused. So, always remember, if someone is trying to teach or preach something and they can't show it to you in New Testament Scripture, then it's junk – leave it alone. The Bible is God talking directly to us. It's His Word and His Word is TRUTH. God's truth is our only safeguard. So, anything you receive must be solidly backed up by Scripture.

Chapter 14 – There's No Limit in God's Eyes

It was hard for me to believe that God wanted everything for me. I knew the Scriptures said it, but it was hard for me to truly believe that God wanted me wealthy, wanted me completely healthy, and wanted me victorious at all times and in all areas of my life. It was difficult for me to believe these things because there was a rotten beam supporting my incorrect belief. It was the way I had been brought up.

Now, I was healthy – totally healthy, because healing was the only thing I studied for years. But God dealt with me one day about how lopsided I was. It was very good that I was healthy, but I was so broke I seriously couldn't leave town. Think about it, how was I going to fulfill my particular call that way? He had plans for me and they were bigger than just that little town.

You see, I had to get my mind renewed in other areas as well. God doesn't want us to be lopsided. It doesn't do us any good to be millionaires but die of sickness because we don't have our minds renewed to healing. Similarly, it doesn't fulfill God's plans if we are as healthy as can be, but be too broke to participate in spreading the Gospel around the world. He wants us to be well rounded and victorious in *all* areas of our lives.

You're No Longer Bound by the Grave Clothes

Lazarus was a friend of Jesus. He had been sick and his sisters sent word to Jesus to come and heal him. But Jesus, at the direction of the Holy Ghost, tarried a couple of days and his friend died. Here's where we pick up the story. Lazarus is dead and wrapped up like a mummy lying in a tomb.

> *41 Then they took away the stone from the place where the dead was laid. And Jesus lifted up his eyes, and said, Father, I thank thee that thou hast heard me.*
>
> *42 And I knew that thou hearest me always: but because of the people which stand by I said it, that they may believe that thou hast sent me.*
>
> *43 And when he thus had spoken, he cried with a loud voice, Lazarus, come forth.*
>
> *44 And he that was dead came forth,* **bound hand and foot with graveclothes: and his face was bound about with a napkin.** *Jesus saith unto them, Loose him, and let him go. (John 11:41-44, KJV, emphasis added)*

Lazarus came out of that tomb, but he was still bound hand and foot with graveclothes and even had the napkin still wrapped around his face! This tells us he couldn't walk and Jesus didn't send anybody in to go get him. Therefore, when Jesus called him out, he was either picked up by the angels or by the power of God. Either way, he couldn't walk, because he was wrapped up like a mummy. Everyone saw him come out of that tomb. There he was standing at the door alive – his life and health had been restored!

Jesus tells the disciples standing around to loose him and let him go because he was still bound in those graveclothes even though he'd been made alive again. I can't tell you how many people we see who are saved and born again, but they're still bound with graveclothes in their thinking. They don't know that health belongs to them – victory belongs to them –prosperity belongs to them –all of these things belong to them. They never get their soul renewed, so they're still bound with the previous life's thinking. Remember, if your thinking is wrong, then your believing on Him will be wrong. And if your believing is wrong, then your talking will be wrong and that opens up a whole new can of worms.

The Lid is Off the Jar

Years ago when God began to deal with me about prosperity, He told me to go look up flea circuses. Now, at first, I thought this was a joke, I really did. I thought I just had too much to eat or something. But, I went to the library and discovered it's true! It's documented. Years ago they would have trained fleas in little circuses. This is true, it's not a joke. You can do a Google search and find all kinds of information about them.

As I was researching the flea circuses, I came across a most interesting experiment of fleas in a glass jar. Zig Ziglar mentioned it often (Ziglar). Most fleas can jump between 12 to 18 inches. Some, perhaps, can jump a little further, but that is their average. They would take fleas and put them in a jar and with a lid on it. The little fleas would jump and hit their head on the lid. Eventually, even though they had the ability to jump higher, they learned they would hit their heads so hard on the lid that they quit jumping that high. The ability to go further was there, but they had accepted the ceiling. After a period of time, the trainer could take the lid off the jar and the fleas would never jump out. For a video demonstration, take a look at the link in the footnotes[104] or do a search on YouTube.

Do you know why so many negative things happen to so many Christians? The devil, by influencing other people, tries to create a ceiling. But, once you are spiritually saved there is no longer any limit in God's eyes. The limit is purely in your own thinking. It is in what *you decide* to accept as your limit.

Believe it or not, while you were being raised, you set a boundary that you unconsciously confine yourself to until you renew your mind to something different and reset the boundary. For example, you may have grown up in a family that struggled financially for generations because you come from a long line of high school drop outs. If you never renew your mind to the WORD on prosperity, then you may, without even realizing it, confine yourself to the boundary of poverty because that's what you are used to even though God has taken the limit off your ability to be prosperous. However, when you start renewing your mind with the WORD of God, you'll start saying things like, "My God shall supply *all* my need! I can walk in wealth *all* the time! I can have victory *everywhere* I go! I am blessed and highly favored!" When you start doing that, you take the limits off! That's unlimited!

Let's take a look at God's limitless resources in action:

> *1 Now there cried a certain woman of the wives of the sons of the prophets unto Elisha, saying, Thy servant my husband is dead; and thou knowest that thy servant did fear the LORD: and the*

104 Training Fleas in a Jar Video (https://www.youtube.com/watch?v=GlpjA-QgmQM)

creditor is come to take unto him my two sons to be bondmen.

² And Elisha said unto her, What shall I do for thee? tell me, what hast thou in the house? And she said, Thine handmaid hath not any thing in the house, save a pot of oil.

³ Then he said, Go, borrow thee vessels abroad of all thy neighbours, even empty vessels; ***borrow not a few.***

⁴ And when thou art come in, thou shalt shut the door upon thee and upon thy sons, and shalt pour out into all those vessels, and thou shalt set aside that which is full.

⁵ So she went from him, and shut the door upon her and upon her sons, who brought the vessels to her; and she poured out.

⁶ And it came to pass, when the vessels were full, that she said unto her son, Bring me yet a vessel. And he said unto her, There is not a vessel more. And the oil stayed. (2 Kings 4:1-6, KJV, emphasis added*)*

You see, in 2 Kings 4, when the widow was going to lose some children to debtor's prison, she went to Elisha the prophet for help. He asked her what she had in the house and she replied that she had only a little oil. It became her seed. In verse three, the Man of God is hinting for her to borrow all the vessels she can possibly borrow. At that point in time, who is the only one that can limit that woman? She is. Jesus has bought and paid for everything we need to live life victoriously[105]. It's unlimited.

---

[105] 2 Peter 1:3

Why not Pygmies Instead of Giants?

Sometimes the limits that we're dealing with aren't keeping us imprisoned or stopping our supply, they are preventing us from moving into the next place God has for us.

> *¹And the LORD spake unto Moses, saying,*
>
> *² Send thou men, that they may search the **land of Canaan, which I give unto the children of Israel**: of every tribe of their fathers shall ye send a man, every one a ruler among them. (Numbers 13:1-2, KJV, emphasis added)*

Before we continue, I want to make sure we are all on the same page. Look carefully, at the second verse, did God give the Children of Israel Canaan's land? Yes He did. Keep in mind that word "ruler" means that these men were all leaders among their tribes. Now, let's continue on and look at their report.

> *²⁷ And they told him, and said, We came unto the land whither thou sentest us, and surely it floweth with milk and honey; and this is the fruit of it.*
>
> *²⁸ Nevertheless the people be strong that dwell in the land, and the cities are walled, and very great: and moreover we saw the children of Anak there.*
>
> *²⁹ The Amalekites dwell in the land of the south: and the Hittites, and the Jebusites, and the Amorites, dwell in the mountains: and the Canaanites dwell by the sea, and by the coast of Jordan.*
>
> *³⁰ And Caleb stilled the people before Moses, and said, Let us go up at once, and possess it; for we are well able to overcome it.*

> *31 But the men that went up with him said, We be not able to go up against the people; for they are stronger than we.*
>
> *32 And **they brought up an evil report** of the land which they had searched unto the children of Israel, saying, The land, through which we have gone to search it, is a land that eateth up the inhabitants thereof; and all the people that we saw in it are men of a great stature.*
>
> *33 And there we saw the giants, the sons of Anak, which come of the giants: and we were in our own sight as grasshoppers, and so we were in their sight. (Numbers 13:27-33, KJV, emphasis added)*

So, here they are just going through the list. They're basically saying, "Yes it's great but there's this problem and that problem." They can't see the milk and honey for the giants! These men came back with stories of how fabulous the land was, but also how great big the giants and the obstacles were. The text shows that all of the men agreed on the richness of the land. But, it also shows that not everyone agreed with the assessment of the difficulty and danger.

That's how it is with the Christian journey. Sometimes, not everybody that goes with you will agree with you on everything. That why, a lot of times, you don't need to tell everybody and his brother everything. If you have a vision for something that God has given you, tell it only to those who will encourage you. Don't tell a bunch of doubters and unbelievers in your life.

So, here these men are all standing around after just being told that God is *giving* them the land of Canaan, and they are complaining about the giants – all except Caleb that is. In verse 30,

Caleb didn't disagree with their assessment of the land. He just believed and agreed with God. Let's look at it in the NLT:

> *30 But Caleb tried to quiet the people as they stood before Moses. "Let's go at once to take the land," he said. "We can certainly conquer it!" (Numbers 13:30, NLT)*

Yet the naysayers in the group wouldn't listen to him. They said, "No. No, we're not able to go up against those people for they're stronger they we are." On our own, you and I are no match for the devil either. But we are not dealing with the devil by ourselves. We are dealing with the devil and the forces of darkness *in the name of Jesus Christ of Nazareth.* We don't have to do this by ourselves.

Verse 32 in the King James says, *"...they brought up an evil report of the land..."* Let's look at that one in the NLT also:

> *32 So they spread this **bad report** about the land among the Israelites: "The land we traveled through and explored will devour anyone who goes to live there. All the people we saw were huge. (Numbers 13:32, NLT, emphasis added)*

Do you see what they did? By bringing up an evil report against the land, they basically lied to themselves and to the people about what God said already belonged to them. When God says that it is yours and that it belongs to you, you can have it. Don't' say, "I'm not able, I can't do that." That is bringing an evil report against what God said is already yours.

If the Holy Ghost is saying, "This is yours. But you need to do this, this, and this to get there." Then you need to do it exactly as He instructed. That is why He says *the steps* of a righteous man are ordered of The LORD[106] – not the benefits, but the steps. Follow each step and you will get there. The 12 spies brought an evil report of the land and look what happened to the Children of Israel.

Look at verses 32 and 33 again. God knew the sons of Anak were there. That didn't surprise God. Many people wonder, if people were already living there, why did God say it belonged to the Children of Israel? Because it did. The people living there had to go. Their time was up as far as He was concerned.

Think of it this way. When God tells you healing belongs to you, He isn't crazy or playing games. He knows there are all kinds of crazy diseases running around down here. They come to *pass*. They don't come to *live*. They go right on by us because we're a bunch of God's favorites! That's how it was with the sons of Anak. Their time had *passed* and Israel's time had *arrived*. They weren't going to have any trouble moving into their land *if they believed what God told them*. The problem was *they believed what they saw* instead.

One time a guy told me, "You know what? Every time I buy something the value of it drops."

I smiled big and said, "Then you're the fellow I'm looking for!" You see, the WORD says I'm blessed going in and blessed going out[107] so I always buy low and I sell high. As soon as I buy something, everybody else wants it.

Have you ever had God tell you to do something and as soon as you stepped out to do it, there were giants all around? Yep. Me too. Seems like every time. They don't want you or me taking

---

106 Psalm 37:23

107 Deuteronomy 28:6

what rightfully belongs to us. There's people living in our houses and driving our cars. Of course, I'm talking about houses and cars that are for sale or will be soon, because we don't go around laying claim to stuff that isn't for sale and things like that.

But, hear me out, if the wealth of the wicked is laid up for the just[108], then I have to have my mind renewed to the kind of thinking that this whole Earth belongs to my Father. If the gold and the silver and the cattle, not a thousand cows, but the cattle on a thousand hills[109] belong to Him and I'm His kid[110], then I'm in direct line for the inheritance[111] and I will have plenty of livestock and houses.

In verse 32 and 33 those spies reported, *"...all the people that we saw in it are men of a great stature. And there we saw the giants, the sons of Anak, which come of the giants..."* So, let me ask you this, why couldn't they have been pygmies or fleas? Because pygmies and fleas don't intimidate us, but giants do. The last part of verse 33 is the key to this whole story, *"...we were in our own sight as grasshoppers..."* They didn't see themselves as the possessors and conquerors[112] God said they were. You're a new creature in Christ Jesus[113]. You're the head and not the tail; you're above and not beneath[114]. You have to see yourself the way God sees you to be able to do what God says to do.

---

108 Proverbs 13:22

109 Psalm 50:10

110 Romans 8:15, Galatians 3:26, and Ephesians 1:5

111 Romans 8:17

112 Romans 8:37

113 2 Corinthians 5:17

114 Deuteronomy 28:13

See Yourself Differently Than the World Sees You

When you meet a stranger, they immediately form an impression of who you are within the first second or two. Mostly, this opinion is based solely on what their natural senses tell them about you before you even speak. Often, this first impression is completely off-base. Let me share an example from my own life:

A friend of mine, Brother Joey, and I were in Kansas City, Missouri. We were headed up to Iowa to preach. My wife had made arrangements for me to get a particular gift. In fact, many in my congregation had given money towards that gift for me. So, Joey and I were traveling in "Old Blue." She was an old blue 1992 Ford F150 with some dents in her, but they weren't whiskey dents. My son, Ricky Jr., had accidentally turned the front end loader loose and it ran over the truck. Anyway, we're traveling in this old truck, but we're dressed real nice. We had on nice jeans and pearl button shirts. We looked sharp!

Eventually, we pull up to this place called *Alaskan Fur*[115] in Kansas City, and we go in. A gentleman with an uncertain look in his eye asks, "Can I help you? Walmart is right down the street."

I replied, "Well that's nice. But, we're hunting something else – a particular jacket."

"Really?" his incredulity was quite apparent.

"Yes, Sir."

---

[115] *Alaskan Fur* is one of the last places where you can buy a real mink coat because there are so many animal activists. You may not know this about me, but I am fully P.E.T.A. Yep, that's right, I fully endorse "People Eating Tasty Animals."

"Well, how exactly are you planning to pay for this?"

"Cash," I answered.

"Cash?" his voice kind of went up a little in his surprise.

He looked at Brother Joey and said, "Sir, you stay right here." Then he grabbed me by the elbow and took me back to the vault where he proceeded to show me all the men's jackets.

Soon enough, I saw the one I wanted and said, "I'll take that one right there."

Later, as Brother Joey and I were discussing this, we realized something very important. To that man, we walked in as Mr. Nobody and his friend, but we came out as Mr. Edwards and Mr. Higgins. It stretched us to realize that you and I, as believers, have to see ourselves differently from how the world sees us. We have to see ourselves as *somebody* because we are! We, *"are a chosen generation, a royal priesthood, a holy nation, His own special people, that you may proclaim the praises of Him who called you out of darkness into His marvelous light"* (1 Peter 2:9, NKJV).

Chapter 15 – The Royal Law of Love

When you and I were saved spiritually, we were instantly made spiritually brand new and right with God.

> *There is therefore now no condemnation to them which are in Christ Jesus, who walk not after the flesh, but after the Spirit.*
>
> *² **For the law of the Spirit of life** in Christ Jesus hath made me free from the law of sin and death. (Romans 8:1-2, KJV, emphasis added)*

"For the law of the Spirit of life…" means life as God has it – the Zoë life. It was imparted into us at salvation. Remember Jesus said, *"…I have come that they may have life, and that they may have it more abundantly"* (John 10:10b, NKJV). Let's look at Romans 8:2 in a more modern translation:

> *A new power is in operation. The Spirit of life in Christ, like a strong wind, has magnificently cleared the air, freeing you from a fated lifetime of brutal tyranny at the hands of sin and death. (Romans 8:2, MSG)*

That sure paints a clear picture doesn't it! Let's continue on with the rest of this passage.

> *⁴ That the righteousness of the law might be fulfilled in us, who walk not after the flesh, but after the Spirit.*

> *5 For they that are after the flesh do mind the things of the flesh; but they that are after the Spirit the things of the Spirit.*
>
> *6 For to be carnally minded is death; but to be spiritually minded is **life** and peace.*
>
> *7 Because the **carnal mind is enmity against God**: for it is not subject to the law of God, neither indeed can be. (Romans 8:4-7, KJV, emphasis added)*

According to verse four, this is a soul that still regards the things of the flesh or what the body wants to do more than what the spirit wants to do. The word "life" in verse six, is the same Zoë life we've been discussing throughout this book (Interlinear Bible).

Now, what does that phrase, *"...the carnal mind is enmity against God..."*mean? Remember, the carnal mind refers to the soul (the mind, the will, and the emotions) that wants to side with the flesh when it is not renewed with the WORD of God. Enmity is an old-fashioned word that mostly means enemy, hostility, and alienation (Greek "2189. echthra"). So that phrase basically means the carnal, or unrenewed, mind is a hostile, alienated enemy of God.

This may come as a surprise to you. But we, as the New Testament Church, do not live by the Ten Commandments that were given in Exodus 20. Why not? Because we were given a new law. James 2:8 calls it "The Royal Law" and it is the Law of Love.

> *8 If you really fulfill the royal law according to the Scripture, "You shall love your neighbor as yourself," you do well; (James 2:8, NKJV)*

Consider this, if you fulfill the Royal Law of Love, you will automatically fulfill all of the Ten Commandments. So, Paul

CHAPTER 15 - THE ROYAL LAW OF LOVE

said that a carnal mind, or soul that has not been renewed with the WORD of God, will still side in with the flesh and will refuse to be subject to the Law of God. Love is the law that governs the New Testament Church. So now, all of a sudden, you've got Christians who really don't want to love one another.

Yet, look what John has to say about this:

> [14] **We know that we have passed from death to life, because we love the brethren.** *He who does not love his brother abides in death. (1 John 3:14, NKJV, emphasis added)*

The Gospel says the world will know you are my disciples because of the love you have for one another[116]. If we aren't walking in love, we need to get our minds renewed, because faith works by love[117].

The Law of the Spirit of Life in Christ Jesus

According to Romans 8:2, *"For the law of the Spirit of life in Christ Jesus hath made me free from the law of sin and death" (NKJV).* The law that governs the Church (and all of Christian life) is the law of the Spirit of life in Christ Jesus. The law of sin and death operates in the world's system, but Jesus said we aren't in that system and the world hates us for it.

> [19] *If you were of the world, the world would love its own. Yet because you are not of the world, but I chose you out of the world, therefore the world hates you. (John 15:19, NKJV)*

---

[116] John 13:35

[117] Galatians 5:6

Once you are saved, if you continue to act like the world, the world will love you. But you have to remember you're not of it – you're only in it. Look at this strong warning about continuing in the old ways you had before salvation:

> 20 *But you have not so learned Christ,* 21 *if indeed you have heard Him and have been taught by Him, as the truth is in Jesus:* 22 *that you put off, concerning your former conduct, the old man which grows corrupt according to the deceitful lusts,* 23 *and* **be renewed in the spirit of your mind,** 24 *and that you put on the new man which was created according to God, in true righteousness and holiness. (Ephesians 4:20-24, NKJV,* emphasis added)

When looking at verse 23, "*...be renewed in the spirit of your mind.*" We need to remember that there is no renewing the reborn human spirit after salvation. It is made completely new and right with God. Therefore, this phrase is talking about the human soul and renewing the mind, the will, and the emotions with the WORD of God. The New Living Translation really brings this out:

> 20 *But that isn't what you learned about Christ.* 21 *Since you have heard about Jesus and have learned the truth that comes from him,* 22 *throw off your old sinful nature and your former way of life, which is corrupted by lust and deception.* 23 *Instead, let the Spirit renew your thoughts and attitudes.* 24 *Put on your new nature, created to be like God —truly righteous and holy. (Ephesians 4:20-24, NLT)*

Ephesians 5 continues to develop this point:

> *¹Imitate God, therefore, in everything you do, because you are his dear children. ² Live a life filled with love, following the example of Christ. He loved us and offered himself as a sacrifice for us, a pleasing aroma to God. (Ephesians 5:1-2, NLT)*

So, God's intention is for Christians to come up above the law of sin and death and operate in the law of the Spirit of life in Christ Jesus and the Royal Law of Love. When we renew our mind to this, it helps us live a new lifestyle from the inside out – one that is righteous and holy.

The Recompense of Reward

God is good. He isn't telling us to live a stand out lifestyle just because He wants to make life on Earth difficult. He has promised us good things will come to us as a result of living our life for Him, and following the Royal Law of Love.

> *³⁵ Cast not away therefore your confidence, which hath great recompence of reward.*
>
> *³⁶ For ye have need of patience, that, after ye have done the will of God, ye might receive the promise. (Hebrews 10:35- 36, KJV)*

Aren't you glad the WORD of God is the WILL of God? I know I am! This means the Church ought to be the healthiest, wealthiest, and most victorious people on the planet. We ought to own all the stuff, because in owning everything, it shows that our God is a good Father in Heaven!

Now people will tell me all the time, "Well Brother Ricky, you know the wealth of the wicked is laid up for the just[118]." They'll believe that, but they don't have anything to their name.

So, I ask them, "Are you just?"

"Yep!" they nod enthusiastically.

"How much you got?"

"I ain't got nothing," they look perplexed.

"So, when you going to get it?"

"I don't know."

Let's get it now! The only way to get it now, is to find out *why* you don't have it. It's one of two things: either you need patience to keep standing firm, or you have violated the Royal Law of Love. Let's address patience first.

Oftentimes, people come to me because they think they need something. They are walking in love and standing in faith, so they say, "Brother Ricky, I need it right now and I mean right now!" But go back and look at Hebrews 10:36, it says after you have done the will of God you need patience so you can receive the promise. He's telling us right here that some things take time.

> *13 For when God made promise to Abraham, because he could swear by no greater, he sware by himself,*
>
> *14 Saying, Surely blessing I will bless thee, and multiplying I will multiply thee.*

---

118 Proverbs 13:22

> *15 And so, **after he had patiently endured**, he obtained the promise.*
>
> *16 For men verily swear by the greater: and an oath for confirmation is to them an end of all strife. (Hebrews 6:13-16, KJV, emphasis added)*

To *"patiently endure"* does not mean you put up with a bunch of junk. No Sir, you are not to allow the devil to run all over you and oppress you. You have to stay in faith the whole time you're enduring. An athlete in a marathon can't sit down halfway through the race and take a rest – he has to keep pressing and enduring to reach the finish line and win the trophy. That's why Matthew 24:13 tells us, *"He who endures to the end shall be saved" (NKJV).* That doesn't mean putting up with a bunch of junk from the devil. It means standing firm and confident knowing that God will do what He says no matter how long you have to stand.

However, there are times when patience isn't the only problem. If you aren't walking in love, then your faith isn't going to work.

> *14 For all the law is fulfilled in one word, even in this: "You shall love your neighbor as yourself."*
>
> *15 But **if you bite and devour one another**, beware lest you be consumed by one another!*
>
> *16 I say then: Walk in the Spirit, and you shall not fulfill the lust of the flesh.*
>
> *17 For the flesh lusts against the Spirit, and the Spirit against the flesh; and these are contrary to one another, so that you do not do the things that you wish. (Galatians 5:14-17, NKJV, emphasis added)*

In verse 15, *"...if you bite and devour one another...,"* he's not talking about leaving teeth marks. He's talking about backbiting, being sarcastic, and otherwise mean to each other (Greek "2719. katesthió"). Now, do you see what's going on here? Having one's soul saved will cause it to side in with the part of you that's right with God; therefore, it will control the flesh. But a Christian who never develops the soul can act very cruel, mean, and crazy – just like people who aren't saved.

Now, let's look carefully at verse 16. He says, *"I say then: Walk in the Spirit, and you shall not fulfill the lust of the flesh."* You have the love of God inside you. Have you ever forgotten that fact, not exercised that love, and acted ugly to someone? You're not alone. What happened? Was your flesh so strong at that moment that it overcame you? No. The soul had to go with it, but as soon as you did it, there was something on the inside of you, the life of God, saying, "Man, I really wish I hadn't said that." See, you know the right way. It's in you, because that's where the life and nature of God are imparted. Don't beat yourself up.

Bumper Stickers and Other Road Etiquette

I drive a pickup a lot. Sometimes my wife will let me drive her car, but for the most part, I'm a truck man. No, I don't have any bumper stickers on my truck. My wife won't let me! She'll never let me put a "Follow me to Family Worship Center" sticker on my bumper. To understand why, picture this:

Remember that "Honk if you love Jesus" sticker from years back? Well, pretend you've got one of those on your bumper and you pull up to a red light. Somebody pulls up behind you and honks their horn. You're like, "The light's red, you idiot!" They keep honking their horn and you get out like, "What? You want some of me?"

"Nah, Man, I just love Jesus!"

"Oh! Me too! I'm sorry..." you have to apologize all sheepishly because you forgot about that silly bumper sticker! Now, imagine you're a preacher and that happens...now you understand. So we're all growing – we're all learning – we're all developing.

That reminds me of another story. I was recently in another state and I left the motel headed to the meeting. Some people were in a big rush, driving aggressively, and cut me off! So, naturally, my flesh wanted to return the favor. But, I'm oh so glad I didn't because they ended up in my meeting! Now wouldn't that be swell? Run them off the road and then get up behind the pulpit and say, "Y'all need to walk in love!"

They'd have been like, "Yeah, you too Brother!" So if you ever see me in my truck and you cut me off, tell me, "I go to your meetings!" before I do anything stupid.

Chapter 16 – The Vine and The Fruit

So Many Words for Spirit

Let's take a look at Galatians 5:17 again:

> *17 **For the flesh lusts against the Spirit**, and the Spirit against the flesh; and these are contrary to one another, so that you do not do the things that you wish. (Galatians 5:17, NKJV,* emphasis added)

Look carefully at that first phrase, *"For the flesh lusts against the Spirit..."* Notice that it doesn't say "Holy Spirit" and also notice the word "Spirit" is capitalized. Many people don't realize this, but in the Bible there are several Hebrew and Greek words for our one English word "spirit" in both the Old Testament and the New Testament (Strong's Search "Spirit"). So, really, unless you look it up in the original Hebrew or Greek, you don't know whether they are talking about the Holy Spirit, the human spirit, a demonic spirit, or whatever. Since you don't know, the translators left off "Holy" but still capitalized "Spirit" as a clue that they are talking about the human spirit and not a demonic spirit[119].

Once you are saved, if you do something contrary to God's principles you know it down in your gut. That's not the Holy

---

[119] www.biblehub.com has a free Interlinear Bible which links to both Strong's Old Testament Hebrew and New Testament Greek Concordances. You simply key in the verse you want to look at, click the Greek or Hebrew word you want to look up, and it will take you to the Strong's entry for the word.

Spirit. It's your spirit letting your flesh know, "Don't do that again! I don't appreciate that." How do I know that is your spirit and not the Holy Spirit? Well, because once you are born again, your spirit is made right with God. It doesn't make sense for your flesh to fight with the Holy Spirit. It wouldn't even be a contest. Furthermore, God doesn't fight or argue with us, because He gave us a free will. The Holy Spirit came into you, into your born again human spirit, where, *"...the flesh lusts against the Spirit and the Spirit against the flesh."* So, if you get your soul saved, your soul will side with you, and then your body's going to have to shut up and come along too.

Your Walk – His Fruit

Now, let's take a look at the second half of that verse and add the next:

> *17 For the flesh lusteth against the Spirit, and the Spirit against the flesh: and these are contrary the one to the other: so that ye cannot do the things that ye would.*
>
> *18 But if ye be **led of the Spirit**, ye are not under the law. (Galatians 5:17-18, KJV, emphasis added)*

Let's unpack what this term "be led of the Spirit" means. The NLT says, *"When you are directed by the Spirit..."* and I really like that because it is very clear. But, confusion can still set in because, in modern America, people talk differently. For example in most churches, you'll quite frequently hear the phrase, "walk in the Spirit" substituted for "led of the Spirit."

Remember, earlier in this book, we discussed that there were nine Fruit of the Spirit[120] imparted into your spirit at salvation. Why did the Holy Spirit bring them? Because they are the life and nature of God. He imparts them into your spirit so that you can partake of Zoë life of God and His life and nature can flow out through you to the world.

> [5] *And hope maketh not ashamed; because **the love of God is shed abroad in our hearts** by the Holy Ghost which is given unto us. (Romans 5:5, KJV, emphasis mine)*

Do you have the love of God in your born again human spirit? Yes you do. It says so right here in Romans 5:5. Brother Hagin used to teach about the love of God and what it is to walk in that love. It is actually walking in the Spirit or walking out of the life and nature of God that was put into you. In other words, it is living life from the inside out. If your soul hasn't been saved, you'll struggle to live from the inside, because your soul will want to go with the thinking or the influence of the world.

> [27] *"I am leaving you with a gift—peace of mind and heart. And the peace I give is a gift the world cannot give. So don't be troubled or afraid. (John 14:27, NLT)*

Do you have the peace of God? Yes you do. So then, from these two verses we see the Holy Spirit brought peace and love along with the other seven Fruit when He came to live inside of you. Therefore, when we see or hear the phrases "led of the Spirit" or "walk in the Spirit" we now understand it simply means to walk by the reborn human spirit according to the things that the Holy

---

[120] [22] *But the Holy Spirit produces this kind of fruit in our lives: love, joy, peace, patience, kindness, goodness, faithfulness,* [23] *gentleness, and self-control. There is no law against these things! (Galatians 5:22-23, NLT)*

Spirit brought with Him (e.g., love, joy, peace, long-suffering, gentleness, goodness, faith, meekness, and temperance[121]) when He came to reside in you at salvation.

Sometimes, people get foggy when they hear someone say, "We got over in the Spirit." That just means they are being led by or living by the part of them that got saved. So, because the love of God was put into us, when we choose to love God's way, we are choosing to walk in the Spirit. That's when we are free from the law of sin and death.

Before we move on, let's take a look at what Jesus said in John 15:1-4.

> *¹I am the true vine, and my Father is the husbandman.*
>
> *² Every branch in me that beareth not fruit he taketh away:* and every branch that beareth fruit, he purgeth it, that it may bring forth more fruit.
>
> *³ Now ye are clean through the word which I have spoken unto you.*
>
> *⁴ Abide in me, and I in you. As the branch cannot bear fruit of itself, except it abide in the vine;* no more can ye, except ye abide in me. (John 15:1-4, KJV, emphasis added)

He said He is the vine and we are the branches. God the Father is the husbandman, or nurseryman in today's terms. He then went on to say that every branch that beareth not, He'll take away. Notice, where does the fruit grow? On the branches. So the nine Fruit of the Spirit must grow on, or through, you. If you are truly spiritually saved and have the Holy Spirit living inside you, then there must be some kind of Fruit showing through you.

---

121 Galatians 5:22-23 KJV

Consider this carefully, no one is perfect. But if there is never any Fruit of the Spirit showing forth, then it is time to start asking some really tough questions. Time is short folks. Don't assume you or your loved ones have plenty of time to take care of this. Appendix 1 has more information on God's plan for spiritual salvation if you aren't sure.

Inheritance vs. Salvation

Brother Hagin taught us at Rhema that so many Christians, especially in the charismatic movement, often struggle with their physical bodies, their minds, their health, and their finances because they live so far beneath what's available to them. He said in the churches he pastored for 12 years, he never buried a church member. He believed they didn't struggle with sickness in the church back then, like we do now, because they didn't struggle with unholy living as much as we do. Why the difference? Back then they knew how to get their souls saved and keep them saved. Today, people are spiritually saved, but they think they can live any way they want, and it'll be ok because they are under grace. But that's not the purpose of grace.

> *19 Now **the works of the flesh** are manifest, which are these; Adultery, fornication, uncleanness, lasciviousness,*
>
> *20 Idolatry, witchcraft, hatred, variance, emulations, wrath, strife, seditions, heresies,*
>
> *21 Envyings, murders, drunkenness, revellings, and such like: of the which I tell you before, as I have also told you in time past, that **they which do such things shall not inherit the kingdom of***

God. *(Galatians 5:19-21, KJV,* emphasis added)

Many of us, myself included, have been taught that people committing the works of the flesh listed in verses 19-21 would be prevented from making Heaven. But that's not what it necessarily means. When you look up the wording, *"...shall not inherit the kingdom of God,"* it literally means, "They shall never possess the things that are available to them for being in the kingdom. They will live defeated lives here on Earth (Greek "2816. kléronomeó")."

Do you remember when Jesus prayed in Matthew 6:9-10, *"Our Father which art in heaven, Hallowed be thy name. Thy kingdom come, Thy will be done in earth, as it is in heaven" (KJV)*? Well, this means we use our wills to access the kingdom privileges and enforce kingdom principles in our lives on Earth the same way they operate in Heaven. In Heaven, nobody's sick, broke, or oppressed. So when the kingdom of God comes, we want it to look that same way here on Earth and demonstrate it to the world, so they'll know we're His kids and He's our King.

But then, those that would do these things mentioned in Galatians 5:16-21, never step over into the kingdom of God living. They are sick, broke, and oppressed. They have all the same kinds of trouble and hell on Earth as people that don't have a covenant. Remember, that's what causes Christians to scratch their head, look at someone, and think, "I thought he was saved. How come he still acts that way?" He's probably genuinely saved, but hasn't spent much time in the WORD and hasn't gotten his mind renewed. If he doesn't get his mind renewed, according to Romans 12:2, then he's still under the influence of the world's system. He's still confined like the fleas in the jar, and doesn't realize he has the power within him to act differently. Christians struggle when they get into hard places because their minds haven't been renewed.

183

I wouldn't be doing my job properly if I didn't go on to tell you this. Everyone must remember, Hebrews 6:4-6 sternly warns us that mature Christians can push these things too far. And if you go too far into a sinful lifestyle, especially if you have been a Minister of the Gospel, there is no way back. Let me assure you, however, if you are reading this book and feel that scratching down inside you. You haven't gone too far yet. Don't go any farther. Don't let your heart grow cold. Repent now. God's not mad at you. He's waiting for you to turn back to Him and come home just like the father in the Parable of the Prodigal Son (Luke 15:11-32).

Premeditated Sin

I say it often, no one is perfect. Even pastors screw up sometimes. The keys to spiritual growth and maturity are: listening to the Holy Spirit, quick obedience, and repentance when necessary. In any given situation, your flesh may not like the outcome, but you'll have the victory nonetheless if you'll use these keys. All of us, even pastors, are still growing and maturing. If we're at this level today, it means God has another level that He's trying to take us to. But, first we have to master the lessons in this level. I'll never forget one of those lessons as I was maturing.

When my wife, Sally, and I still lived in Silsbee we had some neighbors that challenged us. We were pastoring there and had some nice things. We had a swimming pool in the back yard and we'd get it all ready to go and we really enjoyed it. We would come home on Sundays after church and go swimming and sit out by it or something. It was nice. But they had a beam in their thinking and believed, since we were preachers, we shouldn't have anything nice. They were often just downright mean.

I remember there was a chain link fence separating the properties. Well, one Sunday, we came home from church to find our pool covered in grass. Turns out, when they mowed, instead of turning their mower away from the fence, they'd turn toward it. It also looked like they raised the mower deck so it would throw that grass directly into our pool. Well, I let it go and just took care of getting the pool cleaned up.

Then, sometime later, I was gone and my wife had some ladies from the church over for prayer. While they were praying, this guy came over, started cussing her out, made threatening remarks, and waved a pipe around. That was enough for me. When I got home, I grabbed that pipe he left at my house and went straight over to his.

Now, I was a pastor at this time. You have to know, it was premeditated sin because I had gone to my bedroom and put on my Red-Ram steel toe work boots that I wore on the rig. I was fixing to leave a whelp on that guy that a calf could suck. I beat on his front door and shouted, "You'll never do this again. We can't let this one pass. I know better than to rip your door off and come into your house. I'll get arrested. So what I'm going to do is go out into the street and wait for you. Then, I'm going to educate you really good!"

So, I'm standing out in the street and I'm waiting for him and he's up there and I'm yelling, "You chicken!" and a bunch of other stuff. You have to know, at that moment, I was not walking in the Spirit at all.

All of a sudden, the Spirit of God says, "Aren't you a pretty sight?"

"I didn't start it!" I justified.

"Go ahead, you probably can't whoop him anyway," He sighed.

Now that hurt my feelings. Because I'm standing there thinking, "I can do all things through Christ who strengthens me." But you see, I was taking Scripture out of context and using it in the wrong place.

I was surprised by what He said next, "You probably can't whoop him anyway. If you fight him, two things are going to be immediately affected and I can't stop them – your health and your money. You'll be throwing a door wide open; because you are going to violate a law you know to walk in." He was talking about the Royal Law of Love. I knew He was right. So, I had to leave the street, and go to my house without the rout, but I got the victory nevertheless.

Let me tell you, my flesh was so boiled. You won't hurt my wife. You won't attack my family. I don't mind whooping people over that. People gasp and say, "My goodness! You're a preacher! What about the love of God?" You better believe I'm a preacher and good one too. But if the devil is trying to attack my family or my wife, I'm going to hurt him. I'm going to stand up for what's right. I'm going to do what's right. But that day I wasn't going about it in the right way. I was about to sin in my anger and give the devil a foothold[122]. Thank God I applied those keys. I listened to the Holy Spirit when He spoke to me and I obeyed Him quickly.

Now, don't get me wrong, I love humanity, I love people, I really do. I do not want to hurt anybody. When people are having trouble, I love to help them and will bend over and help them do things. But you have to understand that if your soul never gets saved or renewed with the WORD, it will side with your flesh. You

[122] Ephesians 4:26-27

can be a minister like me and still lose control to the flesh if your soul sides in with it.

However, when you keep your soul renewed with the WORD, it will always stay in agreement with the part of you that got right with God. It will keep you healthy because you are redeemed from the law of the spirit of sin and death, and because another law works in our members[123]. The Fruit of the Spirit will always flow from the Vine out through you to the world in the proper manner. You'll be able to resolve conflicts in accordance with the Royal Law of Love rather than sinning in your anger.

---

[123] Romans 8:1-8

Chapter 17 – The Importance of Walking in the Spirit

Walking in the Spirit Brings Freedom

Have you ever been so hurt by someone you hated them for it? Did you think you had lost your salvation because of it?

Brother Hagin used to teach on 1 John 3:14-15 quite a bit:

> *14 We know that we have passed from death unto life, because we love the brethren. He that loveth not his brother abideth in death.*
>
> *15 Whosoever hateth his brother is a murderer: and ye know that no murderer hath eternal life abiding in him. (1 John 3:14-15, KJV)*

He would tell about this lady who came to him frustrated and said, "Well, from what you've been teaching, I don't even know for sure if I'm saved!" He had been teaching about this very subject. But, Brother Hagin knew she was saved, and he also knew there were some hurts and wounds in her soul. Since her soul was not renewed, she continued to carry these hurts and wounds around.

Brother Hagin took her through this whole process regarding the one she had the problems with. He asked her, "Look at me and say, 'I hate my mother-in-law.'" She did. Then he asked her, "What happened on the inside of you?"

"Well, there was something down in there scratching at me," she responded.

"Yes, that's the love of God trying to constrain you. But your soul isn't saved," and he went on to teach her a little bit more.

Soon, she repented and said, "You know what? I see that I don't hate my mother-in-law."

You see, all hurt, anger, and hate sit in the soul. Those painful experiences and emotions do not reside in the spirit where you received God's Divine Nature when you are first saved spiritually. That's why soul wounds can cause so much damage in a Christian's life if they are not dealt with quickly and according to the WORD of God.

Renewing your mind will get you to the place where you realize that you do have the love of God in your spirit[124]. Once you realize that, it is easy to begin walking in love. In fact, that's exactly how the story with that lady ends. A little while later, she fixed a big meal and invited her mother-in-law, Brother Hagin, and Sister Oretha over for a nice feast. As they were sitting around after the meal, she said to him, "I do love my mother-in-law," and she went down the list of reasons why.

Walking in the Spirit Brings Healing

Well, this same couple had three daughters and I believe the middle daughter began to have epileptic seizures. She had been fine up until the age of two. The lady called Brother Hagin and she said, "I know you don't know about seizures, but this is what's

---

124 Romans 5:5

happening. I can tell that my daughter's getting ready to have a seizure. Would you come?"

Brother Hagin said The LORD told him to go, so he and Sister Oretha loaded up in the backseat of the car. They did not talk on the way over. They were both praying and listening for instructions from The LORD. On the way over, The LORD said, "Do not pray for the child nor lay your hands upon the child, but tell the mother, according to the Old Covenant with Israel it says that if you will keep my laws and my statutes and my commandments, I will take sickness and disease away from the midst of thee[125]."

I remember Brother Hagin would tell us over and over again, "If you want to walk in health, you're going to have to walk in love." So, when he got to the house, the child began to have the seizure and he asked her mother, "Are you walking in love?"

She answered, "I am."

So now she's beginning to walk by the Spirit. In other words, she is walking by the Divine Nature of God that is in her spirit. Remember, the Divine Nature is made up of nine characteristics of God which we call the Fruit of the Spirit. She's letting those things flow through her. One of them is love. Since she's walking in love, she's walking by the Spirit. Because of this, the devil had no legal right to oppress her child with seizures – even though he would like her to believe he did.

Brother Hagin told her, "You tell the devil, 'Take your hand off my child. I'm walking in love; therefore, legally you can't touch her.'"

---

[125] Deuteronomy 7:9,15

So, that mother spun around and firmly said, "Devil, in the name of Jesus, you take your hand off my child. I'm walking in love and you can't touch her." Instantly the attack stopped and never came back.

Walking in Your Light

That woman was able to receive healing for her child because she had begun walking in the light of the WORD Brother Hagin taught her. She didn't just hear it. She became a doer of it. We each have to do this. But sometimes, the devil wants to get our eyes off our light and onto someone else's.

As Brother Hagin's student, I would always pay close attention in his meetings. I would usually keep my eyes open and watch him while others were praying. I wasn't being disrespectful. I wanted to understand how he operated, and I wanted to learn how to cooperate with the Holy Ghost. So, I would watch him move in the Holy Ghost when people came up for prayer. Eventually, I began to notice that many times God would have him teach the WORD and then minister to the people.

I would watch him and realize how much knowledge and light he walked in and I'd think, "My goodness!"

But God told me, "You don't have to walk in that light. Learn from him, but also learn to recognize the voice of the Holy Ghost."

I did exactly that. I stayed and learned. Brother Hagin had quite an anointing on him. I'm so glad I don't have to walk in the light he had. I'm only responsible to walk in the light I have. And you're not responsible to walk in the light I have. You are only responsible to walk in the light given to you.

Walking in the Spirit Means Walking in Honor

Elisha was a man of God and a prophet. There was a lady in Shunem who greatly respected and honored the gift God had placed on him. It turns out this honor was very integral to God's plan for both their lives.

> *8 And it fell on a day, that Elisha passed to Shunem, where was a great woman; and she constrained him to eat bread. And so it was, that as oft as he passed by, he turned in thither to eat bread.*
>
> *9 And she said unto her husband, Behold now, I perceive that this is an holy man of God, which passeth by us continually.*
>
> *10 Let us make a little chamber, I pray thee, on the wall; and let us set for him there a bed, and a table, and a stool, and a candlestick: and it shall be, when he cometh to us, that he shall turn in thither.*
>
> *11 And it fell on a day, that he came thither, and he turned into the chamber, and lay there.*
>
> *12 And he said to Gehazi his servant, Call this Shunammite. And when he had called her, she stood before him.*
>
> *13 And he said unto him, Say now unto her, Behold, thou hast been careful for us with all this care; what is to be done for thee? wouldest thou be spoken for to the king, or to the captain of the host? And she answered, I dwell among mine own people.*

14 And he said, What then is to be done for her? And Gehazi answered, Verily she hath no child, and her husband is old.

15 And he said, Call her. And when he had called her, she stood in the door.

16 And he said, About this season, according to the time of life, thou shalt embrace a son. And she said, Nay, my lord, thou man of God, do not lie unto thine handmaid.

17 And the woman conceived, and bare a son at that season that Elisha had said unto her, according to the time of life. (2 Kings 4:8-17, KJV)

This was not a flaky lady. She and her husband loved God and watched Elisha closely to perceive that he was a true man of God. It's important to note that she didn't go out and add this room on to her house on her own. She talked to her husband about it. They were in agreement – they were in unity.

When they built this room, they also had enough sense to know that you cannot buy the things of God. Christians don't lose their common sense when they get saved. In fact, we've got even greater sense, because now we've got the Holy Ghost on the inside of us telling us to do or not to do something. So, we should be able to recognize someone on the TV or radio saying, "Send us $1,000 and we'll pray for you," as a scam artist.

She wasn't trying to buy anything from God or Elisha. She saw he was a true man of God, and she and her husband wanted to honor that gift. Special things happen when we are obedient to honor the men and women of God in our lives. In Ephesians 3:7, Paul said he was made a minister by the grace of God. Then he shares something even more amazing with the Church at Philippi.

> *Even as it is meet for me to think this of*
> *you all, because I have you in my heart;*
> *inasmuch as both in my bonds, and in*
> *the defence and confirmation of the*
> *gospel, **ye all are partakers of my grace.***
> *(Philippians 1:7, KJV, emphasis added)*

The Philippian church honored Paul and gave offerings to his ministry. Notice he says they have a special place in his heart and that those who took care of the man of God are partakers of his grace. Let's look at this same verse in a more modern translation:

> *So it is right that I should feel as I do*
> *about all of you, for you have a special*
> *place in my heart. **You share with me***
> ***the special favor of God,** both in my*
> *imprisonment and in defending and*
> *confirming the truth of the Good News.*
> *(Philippians 1:7, NLT, emphasis added)*

So when the husband and wife wanted to fix that man of God a place to rest and study, the anointing of God on his life moved through them as well. She couldn't buy the man of God. She couldn't buy the things of God. But she could be honorable towards him and obedient to do whatever the LORD told her and her husband to do. In return for their unity[126], obedience, and honor, she was given a blessing more than her mind could accept at first (vs. 16). But of course it was true, at about that same time the next year God gave her a son (vs. 17).

They didn't have a local church or a pastor available to them at that time. So their child manifested through the prophet's office, because that was who was available to her. When you go to a local church, and you have a pastor that loves you and that will teach you. You have the highest ministry anointing available for God to work through. Does it surprise you to hear that the pastoral

---

126 Psalm 133:3

office is the highest ministry anointing? It shouldn't. The shepherd lives with the sheep.

> *But when He saw the multitudes, He*
> *was moved with compassion for them,*
> *because they were weary and scattered,*
> *like sheep having no shepherd.*
> *(Matthew 9:26, NKJV)*

Jesus saw that without a shepherd, people get faint, weary, and want to quit. The day to day battle is just too much for them. They need regular nutrition and attention which does not come through the apostle or the prophet. Traveling ministers are like supplemental vitamins. We blow in, blow up, and blow out. But we shouldn't be the mainstay of your diet.

Walking in the Spirit Brings Advance Warning

Recently, I was praying and meditating while I was traveling. The Spirit of God began to talk to me about a couple that I know. They're partners with us. He began to talk to me about a child of theirs and another child.

Many times The LORD will tell you certain things but He'll never tell you to tell somebody else. If you're a blabber mouth, the Holy Ghost won't tell you much. If he tells you something, you're never supposed to go around telling other people, "Now, I don't want you to tell nobody, but…" He'll quit talking to you in that area if you do.

Often, what He does with me is He'll say something along the lines of, "I don't want you to talk to them about it. But I told you this and every chance you get, I want you to tell him stories, tell him some things from scripture, and let my Spirit deal with him. My desire is for them to come out of that." Finally, a little while later, when my wife and I were on a trip to Arizona and New Mexico, The LORD spoke directly to me and told me to call them and gave me the words to speak to them. So I did.

I called them and said, "I need to set up a time when we can speak on the phone because I'm out of state right now, but I'd like for just you two, not the children, to be able to be there." They agreed and at the appointed time we had the call I shared with them the things the LORD told me to share concerning one of the children.

So we go along there for the rest of our trip and the day I got back, I received a call from this lady saying, "Well, it's already begun..." and she went through a spiel of things concerning one of her children. Then two weeks later, the daughter did something no one would ever, ever dream because she's just a wonderful young lady and everything.

When this all happened, I thought, "You know LORD, it's so good to know stuff ahead of time." You've got the same Holy Ghost that I have and you can know stuff that's out ahead of you too. A Christian can know their future better than a sinner knows their past when they are walking in the Spirit, in love, and in honor.

But God is so good, He talks to everyone, even the visitors, if they're open and willing to listen. Let me share another story to illustrate this:

Years ago, I was holding a camp meeting in Kirbyville, Texas. My wife and I were there to minister the WORD. I remember there was a lady in that service. The LORD had me call her out. Her husband was with her and they came up to the front. She was visiting that church and had just found out she was pregnant. I don't think anyone else knew, because you couldn't tell it by looking at her. Anyway, The LORD had me tell her, "If this means something, you'll know. Don't be disturbed about the report that you're going to get from the doctor about the fact God told you today, if this bears witness with you and your husband. Everything's going to be fine."

Later, she went to the doctor and they confirmed her pregnancy. As the child began to mature and grow in her belly, the doctor told her, "We would like to take the child because it has Down Syndrome." This, quite naturally, shook her up a bit. But aren't you thankful that God knows what is out ahead of us? See, He had already talked to her and let her know that something was going to happen.

Now, she didn't understand a lot of stuff. Remember, she was a visitor that night. She wasn't from a WORD and Faith Church. So, after this report from the doctors, she went back to the pastors from the church in Kirbyville and talked to them. She asked, "How come God told me that ahead of time and said not to be disturbed by that report?"

"Because He loves you," they explained to her. They kept working with her throughout the pregnancy even as the doctors were pressuring her to abort the baby.

She finally told the doctors, "No, we're going to carry the baby." After that the doctors were all doom and gloom. They were telling her it was going to be this way and that way. But you know what? When that baby was born, it was another way! It was whole! It was the way God said.

Chapter 18 – Possessing Your Renewed Soul for Victory

I would like to warn you, that the information in this book is now part of your light. God expects you to walk in it just like he expected the lady to walk in love toward her mother-in-law once Brother Hagin showed her the truth. And, in that, don't be surprised when you are challenged. Just remember, Jesus gave you everything you need inside your reborn spirit and within the pages of The Holy Bible. Possess your soul and walk according to the Spirit and you will not fulfill the lusts of the flesh[127]. It is simple, but not always easy. It is, however, always worth it!

Let's go back to Hebrews 10:39 for a moment.

> *39 But we are not of them who draw back unto **perdition**; but of them that **believe to the saving of the soul**. (Hebrews 10:39, KJV, emphasis added)*

Let's look at it in the Weymouth translation again as well:

> *39 But we are not people who shrink back and perish, but are among those who **believe and gain possession of their souls**. (Hebrews 10:39, WNT, emphasis added)*

Let's take a look at another witness about possessing the soul.

---

127 Galatians 5:16

¹⁹ In your patience possess ye your souls. (Luke 21:19, KJV)

Now, most of us know to talk right. Yet, at the same time, most of us will occasionally need a talk right check up. Even I will occasionally need to reexamine my words. We do this because we are, *"...of them that believe to the saving of the soul" (Hebrews 10:30, KJV).* We also understand this is a process that takes a lot of work and patience in order to see progress. It won't just happen because you sit in church on Sunday mornings.

With the help of the Holy Ghost, many things ought to be clearer to you now about what's going on in your own life, in the lives of your loved ones, and in the Church as a whole. You should be better able to understand why some Christians talk the way they do and act the way they do. Many people call this old-school teaching. They say it is too hard and not current. Nevertheless, let me remind you that anything which curbs sin and helps us to live in greater victory is still current and helpful.

We don't want to be sick like people who don't have a covenant with Jehovah Rapha – The LORD Who Heals[128]. We want to be richer in all aspects than anyone who doesn't have a covenant with Jehovah Jireh – The LORD Who Provides[129]. We want to be more joyful than anyone who doesn't have a covenant with Jehovah Shalom – The LORD of Peace[130]. We want these things because we know that it took Jesus' life to buy them for us. None of us want His death to be in vain for our lives. Those of us who are saved want to go after and accept *everything* He purchased for us. In order to do that, we have to do our part and get our mind

---

[128] Exodus 15:25-27

[129] Genesis 22:14

[130] Judges 6:24

renewed. We renew our minds, so that we will get in agreement with everything He has for us, and so that our soul will line up with our spirit and we can control our bodies.

Some of this stuff that gets into us is so subtle. People think, "Well, I'm saved so I'm OK." As far as making Heaven is concerned, yes, you're OK. But, as far as living victoriously goes, this is an ongoing process. In fact, it will take your whole lifetime – constantly renewing your mind by the WORD of God. The writer of Hebrews said, *"...give the more earnest heed to the things which we have heard, lest at any time we should let them slip" (Hebrews 2:1, KJV).*

When people say, "I just need to die to self." Well, qualify self. Explain what that means. Because when you're spiritually saved, you're good. You're born again and have a brand new spirit. What people really mean when they say that is they need to get their soul saved. They need to continually renew their soul with the WORD, so it doesn't continually side in with the flesh.

Our flesh can't go to Heaven the way it is. The Bible says it must be changed[131]. It can't stand before God the way it is. So we've received the Divine Nature spiritually[132]. We understand that we used to walk according to the fallen nature before we got saved. But those that don't renew their mind and save their soul, even though they are born again and have the Divine Nature in their spirit, will still live by their lower nature. They are just as carnal as those who are not saved.

With the help of the Holy Spirit, we are learning and growing. This is never a message to point fingers at people and

---

[131] 1 Corinthians 15:53

[132] 2 Peter 1:4

say, "You need to straighten up." No. This is a message to bring enlightenment and knowledge. If we desire, we'll come up to it, and we'll walk in greater victory.

Dissolving the Seeds

When we get our emotions right, God is willing to dissolve those subtle seeds of fear, shame, resentment, and anything else that the enemy has planted in our heart. We need only to ask Him for His help. It doesn't matter to God how those seeds got there.

If you are saved and believe you have some seeds you'd like God to dissolve, and if you have gotten your emotions right, you can pray this prayer:

Father, I give you all praise and glory and honor in Jesus' mighty name. I confess that I am saved. I believe Jesus died on the cross for my sins and rose again in victory to sprinkle His blood on the mercy seat of Heaven. I understand that my spirit was made new when I received Jesus' gift of salvation. But, Father, my emotions have been on a roller coaster. I see that there is room to grow in revelation as I learn to renew my mind to save my soul. I commit to renewing my mind each day with Your Word from here forward.

Father God, I let go and release all of the pain and hurts in my soul. Father, right now, I release those who have hurt me in the past. As an act of my will, I forgive them. I let it all go. I'm asking you, Sir, to dissolve any and all seeds of anger, resentment, unforgiveness, and offense which have lodged themselves in my soul. Father, I thank you for your healing power flowing into me right now and healing the scars in my soul as You dissolve these seeds.

Thank you Father for bringing me out to greater victory. You didn't bring me out for me to return. I'm not going back. I'm going on with You, LORD. Father, I thank You that these scars have fled away from me in Jesus' mighty name!

Confession of Victory

This final section is for those who are truly serious about renewing their mind to save their soul. If you aren't serious, it's better for your not to make a confession about it. However, if you are truly planning to work on renewing your mind to save your soul this year, then say this short confession out loud:

"This is the year of my victory! I'm going to renew my mind to save my soul. I'm planting seeds in my mind from God's seed bag, the Bible daily. They will produce a harvest in my life. I will use the keys He's given me. I will listen to the voice of the Holy Spirit. I will quickly obey when I hear and I will repent when necessary. I'm going to govern my lower nature rather than letting it govern me. I'm moving forward with God and not backing up. This is my year of victory!"

You may have had victory last year, but if you'll truly work on this – give it the time and attention it deserves – you'll have an even greater victory this year. You see, when we are constantly renewing our minds, we are being changed from glory to glory to glory[133]. We start looking better every year.

Appendix 1 - The Plan of Spiritual Salvation

Sin is falling short of God's standard and the Bible tells us that everyone has fallen short[134]. The Bible is also very clear that the wages or payment for sin is spiritual death[135] which means eternal separation from God the Father and from love. Let me assure you God does not want to be separated from a single human being and there is no sin too great for Him to forgive if we'll just ask.

Jesus said there is only one way to the Father and it is through Him.

> *6 Jesus saith unto him, I am the way, the truth, and the life: no man cometh unto the Father, but by me. (John 14:6, KJV)*

Why would Jesus say that? He didn't say that because God is trying limit who gets into Heaven. Quite the contrary, He said it because sin demands death and God loves each of us so much that He sent His own Son to die in our place.

> *16 "For this is how God loved the world: He gave his one and only Son, so that everyone who believes in him will not perish but have eternal life. 17 God sent his Son into the world not to judge the*

---

134 Romans 3:23

135 Romans 6:23

world, but to save the world through
him. (John 3:16-17, NLT)

⁸ But God showed his great love for us
by sending Christ to die for us while we
were still sinners. (Romans 5:8, NLT)

Imagine that you are a criminal and you are at court. The judge has found you guilty of a capital crime. The judge has pronounced the death sentence, but the gavel is still in the air – it hasn't hit the desk yet. In walks a man - just a regular looking man and He says, "Judge, I know he's guilty, but I'll take his place. Forgive him and set him free – wipe his slate clean." That's what Jesus did for us.

The Judge is looking at you and waiting for your answer to see if you will accept this man's offer of grace – of salvation. Will you?

The Apostle Paul told us in Romans 10:9 and 10 that all you have to do is call out to Jesus, confess Him as LORD of your life, believe in your heart that God raised Him from the dead, and you'll be saved spiritually or born again.

⁹ If you openly declare that Jesus is Lord
and believe in your heart that God
raised him from the dead, you will be
saved. ¹⁰ For it is by believing in your
heart that you are made right with God,
and it is by openly declaring your faith
that you are saved.

¹³ For "Everyone who calls on the name
of the LORD will be saved." (Romans
10:9-10, and 13, NLT)

If you accept His offer and call out to Him by faith, you will be saved. The judge will not condemn you.

¹ This means that anyone who belongs to
Christ has become a new person. The

old life is gone; a new life has begun!
(Romans 8:1, NKJV)

It doesn't matter how simple the prayer, the very moment a person cries out to Jesus by faith for spiritual salvation, we believe one of the most amazing ***instant*** miracles of transformation occurs. Their spirit is made brand new.

> *17 This means that anyone who belongs to Christ has become a new person. The old life is gone; a new life has begun! (2 Corinthians 5:17, NLT)*

If you haven't already made Jesus your LORD and Savior, take a moment now to do it. There is no time like the present, because we are not guaranteed tomorrow. It is as easy as praying this simple prayer out loud:

> *"Jesus, I believe You are who You say You are – the Son of God. I believe You died on the cross for my sins and I believe God raised You from the dead in victory. I know I have sinned and I repent. I ask your forgiveness. Please come into my heart, save me, and be The LORD of my life. I am yours and you are mine.*
>
> *Thank You! Amen"*

If you just prayed that prayer, we are rejoicing with Heaven right now. Tell someone. Call a Christian friend, call a local church, or even write our ministry office and let us know so we can be praying for you. It is important that you confess your new salvation to someone else to strengthen your faith. Then, be sure to get into a strong Bible-believing church this Sunday. There's a whole lot more great stuff God has in store for you[136].

---

136 Jeremiah 29:11

Ricky Edwards Ministry
P.O. Box 621
Pawnee, OK 74058

Appendix 2 – Whatever You Bind on Earth Will Be Bound in Heaven

In Matthew 16:19, Jesus says, *"...whatever you bind on earth will be bound in heaven..." (NKJV).* What exactly does that mean? The Bible actually talks about three heavens:

1st Heaven = Our Immediate Atmosphere (where we walk and breathe)

2nd Heaven = Outer Space (Sun, Moon, Stars, etc.)

3rd Heaven = The Residence of God (heavenly spheres beyond which is visible) (Stewart)

It is important to understand that humans do not have any right or authority to bind anything in the third Heaven because God lives there. Therefore, the Heaven that Jesus was referring to in Matthew 16:19 was not God's residence or the third Heaven.

Now, look at what Paul said about his own trip to Heaven.

> *2 I knew a man in Christ above fourteen years ago, (whether in the body, I cannot tell; or whether out of the body, I cannot tell: God knoweth;) such an one caught up to the third heaven.*
>
> *3 And I knew such a man, (**whether in the body, or out of the body, I cannot tell:** God knoweth;)*
>
> *4 How that he was caught up into paradise, and **heard unspeakable words, which it is not lawful for a man***

to utter. *(2 Corinthians 12:2-4, KJV,*
emphasis added)

Paul said he was caught up to the 3rd Heaven – that's where God the Father lives. Notice verse three, when you leave this body, you still have another body. That's why Paul couldn't tell if he was in his physical body or in his spiritual body. They look the same!

So, Paul said he was caught up to heaven and heard words that are unlawful for such a man as him to hear (vs. 4). So, what is it talking about? He's talking about the devil getting kicked out of God's residence.

So, going back to Paul in 2 Corinthians 12, Paul is telling us that we don't need to bind anything where God lives because there is nothing to bind there. There is no sickness; there is no poverty; and there sure isn't any devil in Heaven where we're headed. The devil was there once, but that idiot got kicked out, and he hasn't ever gone back to the third Heaven.

See when people read the Book of Job, they say that the devil went up into the Heaven before God and they get stuff all mixed up. But the Bible is clear, he left when Jesus said so in Luke 10:18, and he fell like lightning from Heaven! He never said, "Well, I think I'll leave…" No! He's never gone back before God – ever.

Let's look Ephesians 2 closely:

> 2 *Wherein in time past ye walked according to the course of this world,* ***according to the prince of the power of the air,*** *the spirit that now worketh in the children of disobedience: (Ephesians 2:2, KJV, emphasis added)*

Notice it says we're dealing with the prince of the power of the air which operates in the 1st and 2nd Heavens. Those are directly over the Earth's atmosphere. Spiritual activity in the 1st and 2nd Heavens is what Jesus was talking about in Matthew 16:19. That is what we have authority to come against using His name to bind and loose.

Appendix 3 - A Word for Ministers and Teachers

Brother Hagin always taught us that you can take any truth and push it to the extreme and you'll get over into error. This is an important concept for all ministers to understand.

A few years ago, I had been in a denominational meeting with a group of preachers. I had been teaching about the soul and different things. Afterwards one of the ministers mentioned to me, "You sound like that Hagin guy."

"Yes Sir," I answered, "He was my spiritual father until 2003."

"I heard on his deathbed that he repented of some of the things he taught before he left," he said, but not in a disrespectful way.

I said, "No Sir. Actually, I was there when they took him to St. Francis. I wasn't there the whole time, but I sat with Pastor Hagin and several other ministers that were there at the hospital. Brother David Horton's parents stayed with them to help take care of them. That morning Mrs. Horton fixed breakfast for him and Sister Oretha. When he finished eating, Brother Hagin went and sat down in the front room in his favorite recliner and he just took off. He followed E. W. Kenyon real close and that's about exactly how he did. Well, they all thought it was a heart attack and worked on him for over an hour in his home, but he never ever regained consciousness."

"So, what you heard isn't true," I continued, "But what was taught, what Jesus did bring to him, from what we can tell it was all scriptural."

"Well, I had just heard that," the minister responded.

"I know. You can hear about whatever you want to hear. But that's why we always judge things in the light of the Scripture."

I believe Brother Hagin was one of the most balanced men, as far as scriptural doctrines and staying even, that I ever knew. He wasn't afraid to correct the course when he understood a correction was necessary. For example, three years before he left, Brother Hagin called a Summit Meeting. It was a closed meeting by invitation only. The ministers invited were the ones I consider to be on the forefront of ministry today. He told all of them, "Be careful about money because I can see where we are getting over into error."

Some of the ministers in that meeting got offended because he warned, "Guys you've got to be careful, the reason I'm saying this is you are pushing *a truth* too far and it's getting into error." We believe God wants us all to prosper. When we start driving better cars and living in nicer houses, we know it works. But, you have to know, as a minister, to get up and tell someone, "If you give to us you're going to get 100-fold return," is an edgy statement. By edgy, I mean you could possibly fall off into the ditch.

We don't say things like that in our ministry, because we don't know if the giver is 100-fold dirt[137]. See if someone is holding a grudge and they give me or the church an offering, then

---

[137] Matthew 13:23

212

they aren't doing what they need to do in the area of love[138]. Therefore, that harvest isn't going to grow to its fullest potential. It's not dependent upon who they give to — it's dependent upon their own heart[139].

Remember when Brother Hagin was thinking about giving the blue Cadillac back that he had used his faith to get. Jesus came to him and told him if he did it, that single act would change his doctrine because it would change his thinking and wrong thinking leads to wrong believing which leads to wrong teaching. Jesus said that Brother Hagin's voice to the Body of Christ was too great for his teaching to be off. In fact, he shared that Jesus stopped him on more than one occasion to tell him when he was getting off in some area.

> 3 My brethren, be not many masters, knowing that we shall receive the greater condemnation. (James 3:1, KJV)

According to the Interlinear Bible, the word "masters" here means teachers. This means teachers will get judged more quickly. If you are talking to people and leading them the wrong way, it is better for a two-ton rock to be tied about your neck and be cast into the sea than to offend the babies of the Body of Christ[140]. So, the more folks you talk to the more quickly you'll get into trouble if you are teaching or preaching. Thank God, through the WORD and the Holy Ghost, there's help to get us back on track if we get off.

Keep in mind we're not just talking about doctrine. This is something a lot of people miss. We're talking about behavior too. Ministers and teachers don't just teach with their words. They

---

[138] Galatians 5:6

[139] Mark 4:14-20

[140] Mark 9:42

teach how righteousness lives by how they live. So, the better and more clearly you teach by word *and* deed, the greater voice God will open up for you in the Body of Christ because you are safe. He can trust you not to tell people that He uses sickness to teach them a lesson. He also knows you won't storm out in a fit of carnality if something goes wrong, because you know people are watching.

This doesn't mean you won't ever make a mistake or get mad. But it means that you know how to handle yourself when you are angry and you won't let the sun go down on it. Now, it also means that the more voice you have, and the more influence you have, the better you have to get settled. In other words, you have to get your mind renewed and keep it renewed in *all* areas – not just a few. You need to be well rounded – not lopsided.

Bibliography

"Asunder". n.d. Merriam-Webster. e-Dictionary. 13 April 2016. <http://www.merriam-webster.com/dictionary/asunder>.

"Prosperity". n.d. Random House, Inc. Website. 9 April 2016. <http://www.dictionary.com/browse/prosperity?s=t>.

Amplified Bible. 2015. Grand Rapids: The Lockman Foundation, 2015. Web version found at www.lockman.org. 04 May 2016. <https://www.biblegateway.com/versions/Amplified-Bible-Classic-Edition-AMPC>.

Amplified® Bible, Classic Edition. Zondervan. Grand Rapids: The Lockman Foundation, 1954, 1958, 1962, 1964, 1965, 1987. Web Version found at www.Lockman.org and www.bible.com. 05 04 2016. <www.Bible.com>.

"Biblos Interlinear Bible." 2004-2015. *BibleHub*. Bible Hub and Helps Ministries. Greek Text: Nestle 1904; Variants: {TR} <RP> (WH) <NE> [NA] <SBL>. 15 September 2015. <http://biblehub.com/interlinear/>.

"Carnal." n.d. *Dictionary.com Unabridged*. Random House, Inc. e-Dictionary. 20 April 2016. <http://www.dictionary.com/browse/carnal>.

"Cooter Brown." 12 March 2016. *Wikipedia*. Wikipedia Foundation, Inc. 2016 May 06. <https://en.wikipedia.org/wiki/Cooter_Brown>.

Days of Our Lives. NBC Universal. 1965-2016. Television Daytime Drama. 25 April 2016. <http://www.nbc.com/days-of-our-lives>.

Eugene Peterson. *The Message Bible.* Copyright © 1993, 1994, 1995, 1996, 2000, 2001, 2002. NavPress Publishing Group. Web Bible. 11 April 2016. <https://www.biblegateway.com/passage/?search=Hebrews+2%3A1&version=MSG>.

Girard, Keith F. "States Pour Government Money Into Wine." 21 October 2010. *Bloomberg Businessweek.* Bloomberg L.P. . Journal Article. 6 February 2016. <http://www.bloomberg.com/bw/stories/2010-10-21/states-pour-government-money-into-winebusinessweek-business-news-stock-market-and-financial-advice>.

"Greek "1143. daknó"." 2004-2016. *BibleHub.com.* 31 May 2016. <http://biblehub.com/greek/1143.htm>.

"Greek "2189. echthra"." 2004-20016. *BibleHub.com.* 31 May 2016. <http://biblehub.com/greek/2189.htm>.

"Greek "2719. katesthió"." 2004-2016. *BibleHub.com.* 31 May 2016. <http://biblehub.com/greek/2719.htm>.

"Greek "2816. kléronomeó"." 2004-2016. *BibleHub.* 1 June 2016. <http://biblehub.com/greek/2816.htm>.

"Greek "2962.kurios"." 2004-2016. *BibleHub.com.* 27 July 2016. <http://biblehub.com/greek/2962.htm>.

"Greek "3056.logos"." 2004-2016. *BibleHub.com.* 26 July 2016. <http://biblehub.com/greek/3056.htm>.

Hebrews 2:1. 2014-2015. Bible Hub. Website. 11 April 2016. <http://biblehub.com/hebrews/2-1.htm>.

"Holy Bible, King James Version." 1987. *Bible Gateway.* Ed. Public Domain. Online Bible. 15 September 2015. <https://www.biblegateway.com/versions/King-James-Version-KJV-Bible/>.

"Holy Bible, New Living Translation." copyright © 1996, 2004, 2007 . *Bible Gateway.* Ed. Tyndale House Publishers. Tyndale House Foundation, Carol Stream, Illinois 60188. Online Bible. 15 September 2015. <https://www.biblegateway.com/versions/New-Living-Translation-NLT-Bible/>.

Merriam-Webster. *Merriam-Webster Dictionary.* Ed. Merriam-Webster Online. 2015. Incorporated Merriam-Webster. 10 March 2016. <http://www.merriam-webster.com>.

New King James Version. Nashville: Thomas Nelson - HarperCollins Christian Publishing, Inc., 1982. web-based on BibleGateway.com. 11 May 2016. <https://www.biblegateway.com/versions/New-King-James-Version-NKJV-Bible/#booklist>.

Society, Ecclesia Bible, trans. *The Voice Bible.* Thomas Nelson, Inc., 2012. e-Bible. 23 April 2016. <https://www.biblegateway.com/versions/The-Voice-Bible/>.

Star Wars: A New Hope. By George Lucas. Dir. George Lucas. 1977. Film.

Stewart, Don. "What are the Three Heavens?" 24 April 2007. *Blue Letter Bible.* Web. 23 May 2016. <https://www.blueletterbible.org/faq/don_stewart/don_stewart_151.cfm>.

Strong's Greek Concordance with HELPS - Word Studies. Ed. Thayer's Greek Lexicon. Copyright © 2002, 2003, 2006, 2011 by Biblesoft, Inc. BibleSoft, Inc. 9 March 2016. <www.biblehub.com>.

"Strong's Search "Spirit"." 2004-2016. *BibleHub*. 1 June 2016. <http://biblehub.net/searchstrongs.php?q=spirit>.

Sumrall, Dr. Lester. *Demons, The Answer Book*. New Kensington: Whitaker House, 2003. Book in Print. <http://www.barnesandnoble.com/w/demons-the-answer-book-lester-frank-sumrall/1101968461?ean=9780883689554#productInfoTabs>.

The Living Bible. Carol Stream: Tyndale House Publishers, Inc., 1971. e-Bible. 23 April 2016. <https://www.biblegateway.com/versions/The-Living-Bible-TLB/>.

The New Strong's Concise Concordance & Vine's Concise Dictionary of the Bible. Nashville: Thomas Nelson, Inc, 1999.

"Weymouth New Testament in Modern Speech." Vers. Third Edition. 1913. *Bible Study Tools*. Ed. Public Domain. Online Bible. 15 September 2015. <http://www.biblestudytools.com/wnt/>.

Who was John G. Lake? n.d. Dominion Life Church. Website. 28 April 2016. <http://www.jglm.org/who-is-jglm/>.

Ziglar, Zig. *You Must Be a Flea Trainer*. Ziglar, Inc. Plano: YouTube, 5 January 2012. YouTube Video. 20 April 2016. <https://www.youtube.com/watch?v=Br0BZ-gPSNY&list=PL9SvYxehSISvc8zFBVtHvJU8YK5EuyLKN&index=37>.

BIBLIOGRAPHY